PENGUIN  CLASSICS

ON THE AESTHETIC EDUCATION OF MAN
AND
LETTERS TO PRINCE FREDERICK CHRISTIAN
VON AUGUSTENBURG

FRIEDRICH SCHILLER (1759–1805) was one of the great play-wrights, poets, philosophers and historians writing in German. Penguin also publishes his plays *Mary Stuart*, *The Robbers* and *Wallenstein*. Some of the most productive years of his short life were spent in Jena and Weimar, where his creative friendship with Goethe has taken on mythic status. His poem 'Ode to Joy' inspired the finale of Beethoven's Ninth Symphony and is now the European Union's anthem.

ALEXANDER SCHMIDT is Junior Professor of Intellectual History at the Friedrich Schiller University, Jena, and currently a Feodor Lynen Fellow at the University of Chicago.

KEITH TRIBE has studied and taught at universities in Germany and the UK and is a distinguished author and translator.

T0200963

FRIEDRICH SCHILLER

On the Aesthetic Education of Man

and

Letters to Prince Frederick Christian von Augustenburg

Translated by KEITH TRIBE
with an Introduction and Notes by ALEXANDER SCHMIDT

PENGUIN BOOKS

PENGUIN CLASSICS

UK | USA | Canada | Ireland | Australia
India | New Zealand | South Africa

Penguin Books is part of the Penguin Random House group of companies whose
addresses can be found at global.penguinrandomhouse.com

Penguin
Random House
UK

First published in German as *Ueber die ästhetische Erziehung des Menschen
in einer Reyhe von Briefen* 1795
This translation first published in Penguin Classics 2016

015

Introduction copyright © Alexander Schmidt, 2016
Translation copyright © Keith Tribe, 2016
All rights reserved

The moral right of the translator and the editor has been asserted.

Set in 10.25/12.25 pt Sabon LT Std
Typeset in India by Thomson Digital Pvt Ltd, Noida, Delhi
Printed and bound in Great Britain by Clays Ltd, Elcograf S.p.A.

ISBN: 978-0-141-39696-5

www.greenpenguin.co.uk

Contents

Introduction   vii
Further Reading   xxxv
Abbreviations   xxxix
Note on the Text   xli

On The Aesthetic Education
    Of Man   1

Letters To Prince Frederick
    Christian Von Augustenburg   113

Notes   169
Acknowledgements   181

Introduction

I

Friedrich Schiller is remembered as a poet and a dramatist, but less as a serious theorist of morality and politics. Yet in *On the Aesthetic Education of Man, in a Series of Letters* of 1795 he attempts to solve a central puzzle of republican political thought: how can a free society be erected without plunging the existing social order into chaos when its members are either corrupt or not prepared to live a free life? His controversial answer reformulates a key claim of eighteenth-century aesthetics from Shaftesbury to Kant. It is the fleeting experience of beauty and the development of aesthetic taste that, according to Schiller, allow us to become sociable persons, wrenching us from narrow egoism and from social and material dependencies, which helps us to recognize the freedom of others. This claim in its dazzling rhetorical cast has always provoked strong feelings among its readers. It made *Ueber die ästhetische Erziehung des Menschen, in einer Reyhe von Briefen* a classic work in debates on the relation between aesthetics and politics, from the Romantics to the Marxists and beyond. Many interpreters have read Schiller's essay as a foundational text in cultural criticism, and on the thesis of the autonomy of art at the beginnings of modernity.[1] The intention of Schiller's argument has been a perennial bone of contention. Was the idea of aesthetic education a mere flight from a political revolution gone wrong into an elitist aesthetic utopia? Or, rather, was it an essay in political anthropology, treating political ills at their roots in human nature? Is aesthetic education the means or the ends of the process described by Schiller?

To understand these intentions, as with any text, we first have to ask basic questions about when and in what circumstances the text was written and published. It is important to remember that Schiller attributed a special significance to it among his works. In a letter of January 1795 to Christian Garve, a distinguished philosopher and a translator of Edmund Burke, Adam Ferguson and Adam Smith, Schiller referred to the just-published first nine letters of *On the Aesthetic Education of Man* as his 'political creed', and he regarded it as 'the best [work] that I have done in my life'.[2] By the early 1790s Schiller had already gained some fame as a writer and poet – enough to be recognized by the French National Legislative Assembly as an honorary citizen of France by the decree of 26 August 1792. The decree lauded him, together with George Washington, Thomas Paine, Jeremy Bentham, James Madison, Tadeusz Kościuzsko and others, as one of those who 'have defended the cause of the people against the despotism of kings' and 'with their writings have served the cause of freedom and prepared the liberation of the nations'. This act of political propaganda, staged a few weeks after an Austro-Prussian invasion army had issued a threat to erase Paris, was informed by a rather superficial knowledge of the writings of 'le sieur Gille', to whom the decree merely referred as 'publiciste Allemand'. But the French revolutionaries were not entirely mistaken in their political instincts. Schiller had indeed throughout his main works deeply reflected on the social abuses and the moral corruption of Ancien Régime society. His early dramas, *The Robbers* (1782), *The Conspiracy of Fiesco of Genoa* (1783) and *Don Carlos* (1787), portrayed heroic but often miscarried attempts to rebel against arbitrary rule, privilege and injustice. In the absence of a functioning system of justice, the stage – he summed up his early belief in the quasi-judicial role of the theatre in 1784 – takes over 'the sword and scales and draws the vices in front of a terrible tribunal'.[3]

He knew what he was writing against. Schiller had been born in November 1759, in the midst of the Seven Years War, in Marbach in the south-German Duchy of Württemberg into a middle-class family. From the age of fourteen, the young

Friedrich seemed destined to follow in the footsteps of his father, a lieutenant and military surgeon. Against the explicit wish of his parents, Carl Eugen of Württemberg ordered the gifted student to attend the Karlsschule, a military polytechnic, which the duke had founded recently as a reform institution to breed his administrative and military elite. Schiller's parents were even forced to transfer their rights of parental authority to the duke in 1774. His new 'father', as young Schiller addressed Carl Eugen, was an enlightened despot, widely notorious for his passion for hunting, costly building projects and mistresses. This, together with his Catholicism in a predominantly Lutheran and Pietist territory, was bound to set him on a collision course with the Estates of the country. But Carl Eugen was not prepared to tolerate opposition, putting vocal critics of his regime, such as the eminent jurist Johann Jakob Moser and the poet Christian Friedrich Daniel Schubart, into prison for many years.

Yet despite its emphasis on strict discipline, Schiller received a very modern education at the Karlsschule, which distinguished him from his peers at the Lutheran university of Tübingen. He was trained as a medical doctor but also took classes in state-of-the-art philosophy. One of his teachers, Jakob Friedrich Abel, introduced him to German *Popularphilosophie* as well as French and Scottish thought. Not unlike many medical men of the later eighteenth century, Schiller here took up a profound interest in the intersection between the workings of man's sensuous and moral nature, a theme that was also central to *On the Aesthetic Education of Man*. The relatively new field of philosophical anthropology radically revised in an empirical key some of the established (metaphysical) questions, such as mind–body dualism and the (moral) purpose of man. The Enlightenment science of man drew not only on the observation of human physiology and psychology but also on a comparative and historical study of civilizations and indigenous cultures across the globe. Schiller's doctoral dissertation *On the Relation Between the Animal Nature of Man and His Spiritual Nature*, published in 1780, clearly was a contribution to this wider debate.[4] In it Schiller replaced the traditional dualism of the body and the soul with the up-to-date distinction between human sensuous impulses and needs on the one hand and reason on the other. He thereby sought to refute two major accounts of this relation – both of which could be traced back to schools of ancient thought. The first, somewhat Platonic, position claimed that man's animal nature was a fundamental obstacle to our moral perfection. Hence man's animal impulses and physical needs had to be held in close check both individually and in society. The second was the neo-Epicurean claim that our animal nature was the indispensable means of our happiness and that wisdom and virtue were not ends in themselves but had to aid our physical perfection. Schiller believed that the almost 'fanatical' rejection of this latter moral system in Christian morality was one-sided. Instead, our animal needs and desires provided essential first impulses of man's spiritual perfection of both the individual and mankind as a whole. The young Schiller here agreed with the key hypothesis of Enlightenment historical thought that man's natural needs were what first led to the formation of larger societies, while his artificial desires for riches and power unintentionally drove the progress of mankind to the higher stage of urban civilization and global commerce. He too claimed that intellectual and aesthetic pleasures were conducive to our physical well-being.

Much of this argument was still rather sketchy. Schiller, especially, did not show how exactly our animal nature would be supplanted gradually by our spiritual and moral nature. And yet the dissertation provided a fundamental basis for a nonreligious concern with the intertwined perfection of the individual and the human species, culminating in *On the Aesthetic Education of Man*. Schiller's plays can be understood best as the laboratory in which the poet-surgeon applied the interrelations between competing systems of ideas, human psychology and physiognomy to the life material of human characters.

But his early attempt to establish himself as a dramatist in neighbouring Mannheim proved to be incompatible with his duties as a military surgeon. In 1782 Carl Eugen ordered Schiller's arrest for taking illicit leave to Mannheim and prohibited further literary activities. Schiller fled, returning to his native Württemberg only after the death of the 'old Herod', for a few months in late 1793 and early 1794. Like a growing number of his educated peers he for years led the unsteady life of a writer and journal editor with a fairly small income until he was appointed to a professorship in history and philosophy at Jena in 1789. With his *History of the Uprising of the Netherlands against the Spanish Government* of 1788 and *The History of the Thirty Years War* of 1790, Schiller, like Voltaire, Hume and other Enlightenment literati before him had indeed turned to the lucrative genre of history writing. But despite a massively expanding print market, to live off one's writings alone proved to be impossible for any German author of the time, even the most popular ones. Because of lax copyright laws, literary men in Germany had to follow conventional types of career, seeking positions in ecclesiastical and civil service, or the patronage of princes and noblemen. On the one hand, this institutional integration of the educated curbed political radicalism and established a certain loyalty to the state and its rulers. On the other hand, the literati believed that they formed a new meritocracy, representing the common concern of mankind and the nation. Against an eroding society of privileges based on birth, they claimed prime access to key positions of public life as well as intellectual authority on questions of social reform.

Schiller's appointment to a professorship at Jena was a case of patronage, not scholarly reputation, conferred by Duke Carl August of Saxe-Weimar with the assistance of his ministers Christian Gottlob Voigt and Johann Wolfgang Goethe. It entitled Schiller to a meagre basic salary of 200 thalers. The majority of his income had to be drawn from student fees and literary activities. When Schiller became gravely ill in January 1791, poverty and an untimely death loomed. He was saved from the former by an act of generous princely patronage. In November 1791 Frederick Christian, Prince of Schleswig-Holstein-Augustenburg, a member of the Danish council of state, and Count Ernst von Schimmelmann, the Danish minister of finance and commerce, offered Schiller an unconditional stipend of 3,000 thalers for three years. Misled by a hoax about Schiller's death, they had even held obsequies for their hero in May 1791.

The stipend allowed Schiller three of the intellectually most intense years of his life. He dedicated himself to a close study of Immanuel Kant's critical philosophy, especially the aesthetic theory in the *Critique of Judgement* of 1790. Kant's 'Copernican Revolution' in philosophy had by then become a force of enormous attraction which no serious German intellectual could escape. In his letter to Prince Frederick Christian of 9 February 1793, Schiller clearly recognized this 'revolution ... in the world of philosophy', which called for a new foundation of metaphysics, natural law, politics and aesthetics.

Before Kant, philosophers had been arguing about what was true and false, right and wrong, beautiful and ugly. Now the direction of these questions had changed very dramatically; for Kant asked about the conditions in human understanding which structure our experience and thus allow us to have cognition and make judgements. According to Kant, it is the spontaneity of the human mind independent from the mechanical laws of nature which forms the basis of moral autonomy, enabling human beings to give themselves a moral law, make aesthetic judgements and share a belief in Deity. Kant was aware that this distinction seemed to open up a terrifying gap between the autonomy of laws of reason on the one hand and the strict determinism of nature on the other. How, in particular, could human beings, given their specific desires, diverse needs and physical fetters, be motivated to do the right thing? Furthermore, were only those actions willed in accordance with the prescriptions of the moral law truly free, i.e. accountable actions, while all others remained heteronomous? In the *Critique of Judgement* Kant sought to close this gap by demonstrating how our experience of the sublime and beautiful through art, but especially in nature, was analogous to the freedom and disinterestedness human beings should exhibit in their moral judgements. Whether he had succeeded in doing so has been disputed ever since and sparked an immediate controversy about the feasibility of Kant's philosophical dualism. Many contemporaries believed that he had destroyed antiquated systems of philosophy but, at the same time, thrown up new questions which he himself failed to answer.

Schiller thought so too. By early 1793 he felt confident enough to come up with his own aesthetic theory, expanding on Kant's philosophy but, most of all, addressing some of the central difficulties he identified in it. Literary scholars have accused Schiller of a confused and unscientific use of Kantian terminology in his aesthetics. Yet they ignore that some of the problems Schiller struggled with were inherent in Kant's own dualistic philosophy. Schiller especially wanted to overcome Kant's determination of beauty as subjective, giving it a more objective character, while at the same time preserving key assumptions of Kant's transcendental epistemology. Beauty, Schiller argued, was no ontological quality of an artwork, reflecting the harmonic laws of the cosmos, but the upshot of its 'heautonomy', i.e. autonomous form appearing free from the constraints of the laws of nature. The artwork might, for example, appear to play with the laws of time, space and matter to make them fit its purposes. Kant had grappled with the problem of how freedom as a foundational concept of practical reason could be a subject of sensuous experience. For Schiller, the experience of the artwork would make noumenal moral freedom palpable to us as sensuous beings.

With an eye on a future publication, he discussed his ideas concerning a 'philosophy of the beautiful' in the form of letters which suited a freer form of reflection than a scholarly philosophical tract. Key themes of *On the Aesthetic Education of Man*, especially the relation between moral freedom and aesthetic autonomy, were discussed in Schiller's letters to his Dresden friend Christian Gottfried Körner of January–February 1793, posthumously published as *Kallias, or On Beauty*, as well as in *On Grace and Dignity* from the same year. However, Schiller advanced the actual blueprint of *On the Aesthetic Education of Man* in the series of letters he sent to his sponsor Frederick Christian over the course of 1793. The first letter, of 9 February, announced a theory of art as the main subject of his reflections. But by the second letter, of 13 July, this theory of beauty had become a mere means to a new subject, the politics of reform and revolution.

II

What exactly prompted this very dramatic change of focus is subject to conjecture. With the execution of King Louis XVI in January 1793, the uprising in the Vendée in March and the seizure

of the Convention by Parisian activists on 2 June, events in France
were steering an increasingly violent course. During these years
Schiller was anything but a politically detached, high-minded
spirit, as he was successfully portrayed later. A studious reader
of the *Moniteur*, the leading French newspaper, he could follow
the drama of the French Revolution as it unfolded almost on
a daily basis. He was certainly a reader of *Der neue Teutsche
Merkur*, which the then-celebrated Weimar writer Christoph
Martin Wieland had turned from a mainly literary periodical
into a forum of astute political commentary on the develop-
ments in France. Like Wieland, Schiller had initially sympathized
with the French Revolution but became quickly appalled by its
violence. In December 1792 he contemplated writing a vindica-
tion of Louis XVI and was looking for a suitable translator for a
French version. He even planned to travel to Paris to defend the
king in person in the trial. That Schiller, whose spoken French
was slow and inexpressive, did not pursue these plans saved him
from becoming the protagonist of a tragicomic spectacle.

But there is also an aspect to Schiller's turn to politics in the
letters to the Prince von Augustenburg that is very rarely noticed
in scholarship.[5] It leads us to the other side of the Enlightenment,
the world of secret societies and conspiracy theories. Frederick
Christian's patronage of Schiller is usually portrayed as an act
of selfless devotion to the arts. Yet, as with any benefactor, the
Danish prince had certain expectations of what sort of good his
generosity would promote. Frederick Christian and his confidant
Jens Baggesen, a poet who managed the prince's sponsorship of
Schiller, believed in the moral perfection of mankind through
enlightenment. In their view, the neo-Machiavellian policies of
the absolutist state emerged as the major force of corruption
of human sociability, unable to address human nature and an
obstacle to moral progress. 'The current state-constitutions,'
young Frederick Christian deplored,

> are such that their governments have to make external security
> their priority. To this end all policies are directed, such as the
> promotion of population growth, of industry and commerce.
> This situation does not allow the princes to contemplate policies

which would lead their peoples to the highest degree of morality, happiness and wisdom of which they are capable.[6]

For Frederick Christian and Baggesen, Schiller was foremost the author of the play *Don Carlos*, featuring a dashing, high-minded protagonist, the Marquis of Posa. With Posa, Schiller had created a role model for an entire generation of enlightened bureaucrats. The marquis was easily identifiable as a late-eighteenth-century cosmopolitan republican, who as a counsellor seeks to overcome monarchical despotism and religious fanaticism in the historical setting of sixteenth-century Spain. In his *Letters on Don Carlos* of 1788 Schiller pointed out the moral ambivalences of Posa, especially his readiness to sacrifice his friend Don Carlos in order to implement his political ideals. But this could hardly dampen the widespread enthusiasm for Posa. *Don Carlos* was put on the reading list of the Illuminati, a radical branch of Freemasonry that was founded to bring about enlightenment by exerting secret influence on the ruling elites in Germany.

It is a fitting coincidence that Frederick Christian was eagerly intent on reviving the Illuminati order after it had both been persecuted by the Bavarian government and suffered various internal scandals. Apart from Schiller, he also sponsored Adam Weishaupt, the notorious founder of the Illuminati, who was hiding from Bavarian persecution under the protection of Duke Ernst II of Saxe-Gotha. On 27 November 1793, the very day on which the famous letter by Frederick Christian and Count Schimmelmann is dated, Baggesen drew up a plan for an exclusive intellectual club. Its aim was to promote the moral improvement of mankind and to fight harmful prejudices. Baggesen listed Schiller as one of the possible members and tried to lure him to move to Copenhagen. The plan was never realized, but in 1793 the prince sent Baggesen on a secret mission through north and central Germany to inquire about the state of the 'Phoenix', as they referred to the Illuminati, and a possible reinstatement of the order. Baggesen should, in particular, find out what the order thinks 'about political constitutions and the ways to reform them, what about revolutions?'[7] He was furthermore interested in the effective influence of the order on the French Revolution, a subject of many wild conspiracy theories.

Frederick Christian was an early enthusiast of the revolution. By spring 1793, however, he felt clueless about 'France's great crisis', the future course of the revolution and its very meaning.[8] France was riven by a violent conflict of political factions and actively involved in a major European war with global repercussions. He contemplated migrating to America in case either reactionary or radical Jacobin forces should prevail in the struggle and cast Europe into a new darkness. At this point the Illuminati and the people associated with the order, Frederick Christian hoped, would provide answers about the moral and political future of mankind. In a letter to Baggesen of 8 July 1793 the prince expressed his belief that 'Enceladus' (i.e. Schiller) would be the right person to draw up a constitution for renewed secret societies promoting enlightenment. When Frederick Christian drafted this letter, Baggesen had already spent a few days in 'Memphis', as the two Danes had labelled Jena in the oriental-mystical language fashionable among Freemasons.

Through Baggesen, Schiller was suddenly confronted with the expectations of his sponsor. And he immediately set out to answer the political and moral questions that troubled Frederick Christian as well as a wider group of literati. It is in the light of these questions about the French Revolution and the future of mankind that the (surviving) letters of July, November and December 1793 to the Prince von Augustenburg must be read. This volume, which publishes these important letters to Frederick Christian for the first time in English translation, suggests the need for a closer contextual study of *On the Aesthetic Education of Man*.

The prince could not have been entirely happy with Schiller's response to his perfectibilist ideas and revolutionary enthusiasm. In the July letter Schiller passed an almost Burkean verdict on the French Revolution – and it is worth quoting this at length:

> The attempt by the French people to realize themselves in their sacred rights of man and thereby achieve political freedom has merely revealed their own incapacity and unworthiness, casting not only this unhappy people, but also, with them, a considerable part of Europe, back a whole century in barbarism and servitude.

But, unlike the famed author of *Reflections on the Revolution in France*, Schiller was no defender of the customary and the sure guidance of wisdom coated in prejudice. For Schiller,

> Political and civic freedom remains eternally the most sacred of all things, the most deserving aim of all effort, the great centre of all culture; but this wondrous structure can only be built on the solid foundation of an ennobled character. One has to begin with the creation of the citizens for a constitution, before these citizens can be granted a constitution.

In sharp contrast to Edmund Burke, he viewed the dissolution of traditional society as legitimate, if not a moral obligation. But he rejected it as imprudent in practice. Given the incomplete socialization of its agents, it could only spell evil to destroy the conventional foundations of current society. Where Schiller agreed with Burke was in the idea that politics was about the artful management of man's feelings and passions.

He diagnosed a profound practical failure of the theoretical culture of the Enlightenment in addressing man's mixed nature of reason and the senses. In social terms, it had proven unable to reach out to the socially disadvantaged, whose political liberation had led to lawless licence. Even worse, among the educated and privileged, enlightenment had brought about a cynical impotence to act according to the law of reason and to do the right thing. Here, on Schiller's account, aesthetic education would fulfil a twofold function. On the one hand, it would free us (through the relaxing effects of beauty) from the immediacy of uncultivated instincts, moderate our passions and help develop our reflective faculties. On the other hand, it would invigorate our will in the experience of the sublime.

The very idea of aesthetic education has grown into an emblem of a morally high-minded utopianism, political or anti-political – in any case, an alternative to robust political realism. But as the letter of 3 December 1793 to the Prince von Augustenburg clearly demonstrates, Schiller toyed with his own version of a morality that was aimed at serving political purposes. In line with a number of enlightened thinkers, Schiller claimed that our faculty of taste is bound up with an outward-looking concern for the conventions of society. Taste submits our passions to the soft force of etiquette, enforcing a legalistic morality or secondary socialization. Like religion, it can thus function as a surrogate for genuine moral goodness, i.e. action according to a moral will, in supporting peace and the workings of society. This was, in any case, very different from Frederick Christian's rationalist optimism that fighting social and religious prejudices would promote human progress and freedom.

When a fire in the castle of Christiansburg on 26 February 1794 destroyed the original letters, Schiller thoroughly redrafted his own copies for publication. They appeared under the title of *On the Aesthetic Education of Man, in a Series of Letters* in three early issues of Schiller's journal *Die Horen* from January to June 1795. Schiller stated the journal's aims in the advance publicity for *Die Horen* in December 1794. Amidst partisan controversies about the French Revolution and the ensuing wars with revolutionary France, *Die Horen*, Schiller wrote, was to provide a safe haven for debate, in which Germany's finest minds – such as Goethe, Herder, Jacobi, Fichte and the Humboldt brothers – would reflect on issues of universal interest.[9] As early reviewers of *Die Horen* recognized, *On the Aesthetic Education of Man* was the most eminent contribution to this journal, formulating its core ideological contention that the public had to dedicate greater attention to fundamental philosophical and aesthetic issues in order to overcome the deadlocked situation of current politics.

III

The grand theme of *On the Aesthetic Education of Man* grappled with a problem that troubled nearly every thinker of note in the age of the French Revolution: how can the society of the Ancien Régime be transformed in order to allow for greater civil liberty? Was this a process which had to be initiated from the highest echelons of society or from the bottom up? What was the exact role of the growing educated middle class in this transformation?

Some of Schiller's closest acquaintances in Jena, including Johann Gottlieb Fichte, Wilhelm von Humboldt and Karl Leonhard Reinhold, sought to answer these questions along the lines of a gradual self-enforcing maturation of inner and outer freedom that would propel a profound reform process. In *The Limits of State Action* of 1792, Wilhelm von Humboldt claimed that the gradual removal of state fetters would tap the autonomous energies of each individual citizen and the nation as a whole, which in return allowed for a further lessening of state interference.[10] 'A certain degree of political freedom suffices to prompt a certain degree of outer freedom of conscience and thinking, which would then permit a higher degree of political freedom,' claimed Reinhold, a prominent Kantian philosopher, friend of Baggesen and member of the Illuminati order, in 1792.[11] Political freedom, on Reinhold's account, was hence prompted by cultural progress. But the stage of civilization achieved in Europe's most advanced country, France, was mainly one of material refinement based on luxury production, not moral progress. The lower classes lingered in ignorance, while a blasé decadent nobility had only deserved to be toppled and stripped of its privileges. In addition, a materialist morality had sapped the moral energies of the middle classes, preventing them from taking the leading role in society. This diagnosis of the social shortcomings of the revolution in France was a recurring theme among anti-revolutionaries, such as Edmund Burke, but it was also elaborated by some supporters of the revolution such as Mary Wollstonecraft, who wrote that the French national character had not been ripe for such a fundamental political transformation. Schiller shared this position in the letter to the Prince von Augustenburg of 13 July 1793 and in the Fifth Letter of *On the Aesthetic Education of Man*.

By the end of 1794, however, the political situation in France had stabilized. The new Thermidorian regime was about to rebuild the French republic and to conclude the peace treaty of Basle with Prussia, which turned north Germany (including Saxe-Weimar) into a peace zone and prompted Kant to contemplate a perpetual peace safeguarded by a federation of republics. An article in Wieland's *Der neue Teutsche Merkur* in early 1795 lauded the attempts by the new French government to restore the arts and sciences as means to combat the brutalization of society.[12] Viewed in this context, it would be a gross simplification to interpret *On the Aesthetic Education of Man* merely as Schiller's response to the Jacobin Terror or to the French Revolution in general, as it is repeatedly claimed in much of the scholarly literature. Rather, *On the Aesthetic Education of Man* can be read as an anthropological complement to Kant's *Towards Perpetual Peace* of the same year. Kant's essay was about securing peace between states as a prerequisite for the moralization of society. Schiller's text essentially aimed at the same, but through overcoming the antagonism both within the individual and between individuals in society. He now dropped his specific polemics against the French Revolution from the letters to the Prince von Augustenburg in favour of a more universal analysis of the meagre prospects for any radical transformation of current human society. In a staggeringly dense form, Schiller employed here key elements of Enlightenment conjectural histories of mankind, moral philosophy and anthropology. In line with Rousseau's prophetic *Discourse on the Origins of Inequality* of 1755 and Kant's philosophy of history, he diagnosed a profound paradox that lay at the core of the historical trajectory of a modern society based on a division of ranks and specialization. Mankind had progressed at the expense of man's autonomous moral agency.

An influential theory among enlightened thinkers, especially Scots such as David Hume and Adam Smith, portrayed the rise of civil liberties in modern Europe as the result of the often unintended consequences of self-interest, commercial progress and the accompanying shift of property relations in favour of the rising middling ranks of society. In his earlier historical writings, Schiller had employed key elements of this narrative. In *On the Aesthetic Education of Man*, however, he identified central difficulties in both commercial progress and political revolution, thereby drawing heavily not only on the gloomier aspects of the Scots' analysis of the effects of the division of labour on civil society but also on Rousseau and Kant. Schiller agreed with Adam Ferguson and Kant that the expansion of man's needs, his unsociable drive for riches and social distinctions, had propelled civilization, awakened human freedom from mere animality and thus produced the material and intellectual conditions for a morality guided by reason alone. But Kant struggled with the problem of how the crooked timber of mankind would be able to progress from the conventionalism of mere external refinement or secondary socialization to autonomously embraced moral goodness. Furthermore, wasn't modernity characterized by a cosmopolitan moral sentimentalism, catering for our self-love, but unaccompanied by action?

Both Kant and Schiller took seriously Rousseau's critique of sociality in commercial society as deeply tarnished by the masquerades of inflamed *amour propre*, which aims at the increase of our social capital at the expense of others. The human need for social recognition thereby became the source of a subtle enslavement of the self. As Schiller puts it in the Fifth Letter:

> Egoism has established its system at the heart of the most elaborated sociability, and in the absence of its very own sociable heart we experience all the contagion and affliction of society. We subordinate our free judgement to the despotic opinion of society, our feeling to its bizarre customs, our will to its seductions – it is only our impulsiveness that we maintain in the face of its divine laws. A complacent egoism seizes the heart of the man of the world, a heart that in the primitive natural man often beats in sympathy . . .

Schiller identified a profound alienation in human nature prompted by the progress of civilization. The division of labour had brought about a dramatic specialization in society as well as a sharp separation of human faculties within the individual, turning every human being into a small cog in an enormous machine. Among the social elites modern refinement had merely masked and intensified man's unsociable qualities into a boredom ripe with malice, as depicted in Pierre Choderlos de Laclos's scandalous epistolary novel *Dangerous Liaisons*. Furthermore, as Schiller made clear in the letter of 11 November 1793 to the Prince von Augustenburg, large parts of society were still excluded from material progress and thus unable to participate in enlightenment.[13]

The Fifth and Sixth Letters have come to be seen as somewhat of a *locus classicus*, almost an archetype of cultural critique. But this reading misses Schiller's main point. For his analysis is as much about the state as it is about culture. The question *On the Aesthetic Education of Man* addresses, especially the first nine letters, is to what extent a stable political community can be erected and upheld by selfish individuals – Kant's famous 'people of reasonable devils'.[14] Hence, to what extent can morality be separated from politics and law in a republic? Like Rousseau, Schiller was rather sceptical about such a sharp division. *On the Aesthetic Education of Man* here rephrased a commonplace of the republican tradition in political thought: political liberty cannot be achieved straightaway by a people morally corrupted by political oppression and dependency. The Sixth Letter blamed the modern form of bureaucratic government of the machine-state for turning its members into functional elements as tax-payers and into administrators through social statistics and numerous regulations. Yet functional effectiveness could not compensate for lack of legitimacy and consent. The government would become further detached from its subjects, leading to a collapse of political authority. The prediction of the Sixth Letter was unequivocal: 'positive society relapses into a moral state of nature'. Rescue could hence not be expected from the current 'barbaric state'. It was part of the problem, not of the solution.

Schiller was no naive adherent of the notion of an original contract forged by rational, free individuals in a supposed state of nature. He rejected it as fictitious. Man in most parts of the world would find himself in a *Naturstaat*, an almost Hobbesian absolutist state built on mere force, and erected to quell his unsociable qualities and to satisfy his physical needs. But these functions of the *Naturstaat* were insufficient with respect to us as free moral beings. It could hence be legitimately overthrown. The aim was the *Vernunftstaat* (the state of reason), built with the free will of its citizens. In line with a voluntarist tradition in political thought, especially of Rousseau in the *Social Contract* of 1762, Schiller claims in the Fourth Letter that the state should express and represent the moral volition of its members. But, as Patrick Riley has pointed out, the voluntarist element of this line of political thought was riddled with serious difficulties.[15] And it is only in response to these difficulties that we can fully grasp the idea of aesthetic education. 'Will' comprised two notions in early modern moral philosophy. The first signified a mere appetite, the last element in a chain of physical causes connected to the deliberation of our reason and impulses. The second denoted will in a moral or an elective sense. Schiller, like Rousseau, wishes the state to embody some sort of virtuous social life through the moral will of its members. Yet how could one be sure that the sum of individual, and potentially egoist, wills would really amount to the common good? As pointed out above, Schiller viewed individuals in modern society as disconnected, insufficiently cultured and driven by social antagonism.

By contrast, the pursuit of the common good and a free life were deeply connected in Greek and Roman republican thought. Its tradition, however, was little concerned with the individual moral will and individual consent. Schiller, like Rousseau, admired the unity of the citizenly way of life of the ancient republics, even if he, in sharp contrast to Rousseau, preferred the Athenian republic created by the legislation of Solon to the austerity of the Sparta of Lycurgus.[16] To be sure, Schiller was under no sentimental illusions that the liberty of the ancient Athenians built on slavery could ever be restored straightforwardly in commercial modernity, where the antagonism of unsociable sociability was the essential component of material and intellectual progress. The ancient notion of citizenship was that of an exclusive nature incompatible with the modern idea of universal human freedom.[17] Yet, rather like Rousseau and Hegel, Schiller sought to combine some elements of the organic cohesiveness of ancient republics with modern individual voluntarism in his notion of the state:

> But since the state should be an organization that creates itself for itself, it can only be realized if the parts have been attuned to the idea of the whole. Because the state represents the pure and objective humanity in the hearts of its citizens, it will have to observe with respect to its citizens the same relationship as each has to himself, and will be able to honour their subjective humanity only to the extent that it is refined into objective humanity.

This emphasis in the Fourth Letter on the organic expression of the moral will of the individual in the moral person of the state takes up key elements from Rousseau's concept of the general will in the *Social Contract*. To bring about self-determination through the rule of law in the *Vernunftstaat*, it was essential to transform the hearts and minds of its members. Schiller's moral perfectionism shared with Rousseau an emphasis on socialization that would sublate egoism as the source of individual and collective enslavement. Only if we take this seriously can we understand why he emphasized the formation of character as a means to political reform. But, as Riley has pointed out, Rousseau's theoretical attempt to generalize the individual will by means of civic education and the legislation of wise men implied a serious difficulty.[18] It threatened to obliterate the empirical autonomy of individuals through force and manipulative strategies that were meant to transform self-love into a source of public good, such as in patriotic self-sacrifice or female chastity. Schiller identified a similar threat of heteronomous suppression of man as a sensuous being (not a merely rational entity) in Fichte's moral perfectionism. According to Fichte, it was part of our moral calling to control our sensuous nature rigorously in order to make it serve our rational perfection both individually and collectively as mankind. Fichte had laid out this moral rigorism in his extremely popular Jena lectures *On the Vocation of the Scholar* of 1794. In one of the few instances where Schiller explicitly refers to a published work, he answers his colleague's rationalist call for moral unity with his notion of moral perfectionism that would preserve the autonomy of man as a mixed being of reason and the senses:

> This pure man, visible more or less clearly in every subject, is represented by the state: the objective and also canonical form in which the diversity of subjects seeks unity. Now there are two distinct ways in which we might imagine how temporal man coincides with the idea of man, and just as many ways in which the state can manifest itself in individuals: either through the pure man suppressing empirical man (the state suppressing individuality), or by the individual *becoming* the state (temporal man *refining* himself into the idea of man).

IV

But why did Schiller so ardently make the case for aesthetic education as the means to realize a free society, discarding implicitly governmental reform, religion or enlightened moral education? And in what sense was the process of balancing rational and sensuous human nature outlined in the *Letters* an 'education' in any conventional sense? With this tract Schiller had, rather late in the day, entered the arena of an extensive debate about the role of the arts in moral and civic education that occupied some of the finest minds in the eighteenth century. To understand the originality of *On the Aesthetic Education of Man*, its seemingly paradoxical emphasis on aesthetic autonomy as the key instrument informing moral autonomy, it is vital to recover some of the outlines of this discourse.

Human capacity to experience beauty and the sublime had been a central reference point in eighteenth-century attempts to rescue morality and man's sociable inclinations as a solid basis of society from the attack of what Hume famously termed the 'selfish hypothesis'.[19] What fascinated thinkers from the Third Earl of Shaftesbury to Schiller about aesthetic experience was the independence of the pleasure we take in it from considerations of personal advantage. In a relatively late contribution to the debate, Kant put disinterestedness at the core of a judgement of beauty, disconnecting it from a judgement of utility. Beauty was the 'symbol of morality', Kant claimed in an often cited phrase.[20] Aesthetic response thus points at a quality in human nature which is immune to the egoistic pursuit of honour and profit prompted by our self-liking and *amour propre* in polite societies and depicted unsparingly by Rousseau and other moralists.

The exact relationship between the fine arts as social expressions and morality, however, was the subject of fierce controversy, not least since Rousseau had infamously claimed in 1750 that the fine arts were the upshot of morally destructive luxury and hence incompatible with republican virtue. And Kant asserted that it was the experience of the sublime in nature rather than the mere pleasures of artistic beauty that could inspire moral feelings. As Michael Sonenscher observes, the debate about the arts here was structured by a polarity between two concepts of civilization: 'For the first, the arts polished and embellished primitive human nature, while for the second, they were real evidence of humanity's original natural dignity. One, put very crudely, pointed to the value of culture. The other, put equally crudely, pointed to the value of nature.'[21] The question was hence: could the fine arts promote genuine virtue or merely function as polite surrogates of morality in managing socially hazardous passions of fallen men who could never be restored to goodness?

In the preface of his influential *General Theory of the Fine Arts*, Johann Georg Sulzer, a Prussian-Swiss philosopher, opposed Rousseau, outlining how aesthetics and morals would work in tandem in human education:

> From a repeated consumption of pleasure in the beautiful and the good arises a desire for it, and from the repulsive effect, which the ugly and the evil impresses upon us develops a repugnance against everything which is against the moral order. Through this desire and this repugnance the human being is stirred to a noble readiness to act (*Würksamkeit*), which engages tirelessly in the promotion of the good and the prevention of evil.[22]

These moralizing effects of the fine arts were at the heart of the political programme of many Christian and republican political thinkers. They hoped that aesthetic education would form the basis of civic patriotism and remedy the deep inequalities of a society based on ranks of birth and wealth. 'The separation of men into different classes,' Henry Home, Lord Kames, contends in the *Elements of Criticism* of 1762 (a work Schiller engaged with in its German translation),

> by birth, office, or occupation, however necessary, tends to relax the connection that ought to be among members of the same state; which bad effect is in some measure prevented by the access all ranks of people have to public spectacles, and to amusements

that are best enjoyed in company. Such meetings, where every
one partakes of the same pleasures in common, are no slight support to the social affections.[23]

In his dedicatory epistle to King George III, the Scottish advocate warned of the baneful dialectics of empire and wealth,
threatening the moral foundations of the British Union through
the corrupting effects of luxury on *amor patriae* and morals.
Lord Kames suggested that opulence be diverted from harmful
luxury into the fine arts, in order to promote virtue and social
cohesion on the model of ancient Greece.[24]

The opponents of a high-flying neoclassical patriotism such
as Voltaire, by contrast, emphasized the role of the fine arts in
emancipating mankind from barbarism and intolerance. In light
of the experience of past religious wars, they especially viewed
the polite pleasures of the fine arts as a psychological antidote
against socially destructive sectarian fanaticism as well as an
ideologically much less risky medium of social harmonization
than the religion of the Churches. According to Adam Smith,

> The state, by encouraging, that is by giving entire liberty to all
> those who for their own interest would attempt, without scandal
> or indecency, to amuse and divert the people by painting, poetry,
> musick, dancing; by all sorts of dramatic representations and
> exhibitions, would easily dissipate, in the greater part of them,
> that melancholy and gloomy humour which is almost always the
> nurse of popular superstition and enthusiasm.[25]

In the *Letters to Prince Frederick Christian von Augustenburg*
and *On the Aesthetic Education of Man*, Schiller drew on this
idea that the psychologically relaxing effects of the arts would
help to dispel revolutionary furore. Schiller ingeniously synthe-
sized the debate between neo-republican and polite positions on
the social role of the fine arts along the lines of the distinction
between the sublime and the beautiful in eighteenth-century
aesthetics. 'Liquifying beauty' would civilize and refine, while
the effects of the sublime or 'energetic beauty' would moralize
and activate virtue. Taking his social diagnosis into account,

Schiller came up with a prescription mirroring a twofold social typology. First, the intellectually refined social elite, whose insights do not comply with its actions – Schiller uses the term 'barbarian' here – needed the strengthening effects of energetic beauty (or the sublime) in order to regain moral vigour. Second, the uneducated classes, who are merely restrained by force, the 'savages', needed the relaxing influence of liquifying beauty to cultivate and check their affects and natural needs.

Nevertheless, he rejected the moralization of the content of the artwork as a certain recipe for the creation of bad art.[26] Schiller discarded the emphasis on the moralizing content of art; but he did not discard the relation between freedom and art. This freedom, however, is realized less through the actual content than via the form of the artwork itself.

V

Schiller develops an aspirational vision of how aesthetic experience would transform the unsociable foundations of current society into a sociable one, constituted by the fundamental law *'to give freedom by means of freedom'* (Twenty-seventh Letter). Throughout the essay Schiller adapts, and sometimes confusingly mixes, various idioms from aesthetics, psychology, legal, moral and political thought. In line with early modern natural law thinking, which goes back to Hugo Grotius and Samuel Pufendorf, this letter revises the idea of sociality (*socialitas*) as a (moral) obligation to treat others as bearers of rights and obligations. This involves a certain reciprocity and an ability to switch roles in one's imagination. Schiller, however, is confronted with a specific difficulty. He does not believe in a naturally sociable character in mankind.[27] Hence the resources in human nature to support this moral obligation and to act accordingly are extremely sparse.

In a move of philosophical conjecture, very much like Rousseau in the *Discourse on the Origins of Inequality*, Schiller denies original man the ability to sympathize with other human beings and with it the notion of self-consciousness.

Instead, in the Twenty-fourth Letter he is merely concerned with self-preservation and the satisfaction of primitive needs: 'Eternally uniform in his aims, eternally capricious in his judgements, self-obsessed without ever being properly himself, footloose without being free, a slave without a rule to follow.' Following Rousseau precisely, Schiller states that the perfection of human faculties, especially the development of reason and imagination, led only to a multiplication of human needs and hence human sorrows. Reason, at this stage, did not develop as a remedy for human suffering. Instilling primitive fellow-feeling and awareness of future needs, reason emancipates mankind from life in the moment. But this creates a sense of nature as an inimical environment threating human beings with many wants. Furthermore, human beings project their own need-driven egoism onto other human beings, viewing them as competitors and potential enemies. Schiller here takes up the cognitive feature key to Hobbes's radical version of the concept of a state of nature in its Rousseauean version with its emphasis on artificial, i.e. imagined, needs as the sources of social antagonism. He thereby strictly sidelines any anthropological account which emphasizes man's sociable features such as parental love. Schiller makes clear that both this evolutionary model and the antagonistic state of nature are philosophical hypotheses which cannot be found empirically in a pure form. Yet they help explain the centrality of the aesthetic in emancipating us from the immediate determination of needs, both natural and artificial, transforming the human being from an animal to a moral person. When he wrote (at the beginning of the Twenty-sixth Letter) that the emancipating aesthetic mood 'has to be a gift of nature; only the favour of chance can loosen the fetters of the original physical condition, and lead the savage to beauty', every informed eighteenth-century reader would have understood what Schiller was getting at. No divine intervention or providence was involved in the natural history of aesthetic education. It was entirely a product of natural chance and autonomous human culture. Empirically, the human drive to embellishment and decoration, which can already be found at a very primitive stage of civilization,

demonstrates the emancipation of man from nature in the artwork which preserves us as sensuous beings.

This recapitulation of the anthropological argument of the
final letters of *On the Aesthetic Education of Man* clarifies
why Schiller took such great, and, as some commentators
argue, unsuccessful, pains in the Eleventh to Twenty-second
Letters to develop a transcendental deduction of aesthetic
beauty as intermediary force or middle state, which evolves
from the interplay between the passivity of the material
impulse and the activity of the formal impulse, between our
senses and reason. He thereby argued that a suppression of
our natural inclinations for the sake of the autonomy of our
moral judgement would not make man fully free. Schiller followed his Jena colleague Reinhold in addressing a specific
problem in Kant's notion of the will.[28] According to Kant's
practical philosophy, the will is fully free insofar as it is
autonomous, i.e. when gives itself a moral law in accordance
with reason and independently from natural causes. But, as
Reinhold pointed out in 1792, this identification of morality with freedom amounts to a circular deduction of freedom
from morality. The implication is that immoral or morally
questionable actions are, in a strict sense, not performed freely
and accountably. Kant (later) sought to solve the practical
problem involved by strictly distinguishing between external
or legal and political freedom on the one hand and internal or
moral freedom on the other. But not everyone was convinced
by such a sharp distinction between morality and legality.
As an early admirer and critic of Kant, Reinhold developed
a triadic model of human nature in which the will forms a
middle or neutral power between the selfish impulse and the
altruistic impulse.[29]

Reworking Reinhold, Schiller sketched out two notions of
freedom.[30] One followed the Kantian notion of a free and spontaneous (moral) reasoning. But, as Schiller made clear in line
with the Christian Augustinian notion of the will, this moral
freedom can be prevented from fully realizing its capacities in
the world by our physical and sensuous nature, our passions
and impulses. He thus proposed a second notion of freedom, in

which our sensuous nature is not suppressed by but reconciled with our intellect.

According to Schiller, aesthetic experience is characterized by a constant interplay between the senses and cognition, material and form. Through this temporary state, volition is taught how to take a distance from the immediacy of our needs and of the sensuous in the realm of appearance without forcing human feelings. This playful distance, Schiller claims, is the root of the development of reflection and thus reason. In terms of psychology, we can experience this equilibrium in what Schiller calls the aesthetic state of our psyche, where we are determined neither by sensation nor by reason. He thereby concedes to potential critics that beauty produces no particular intellectual or moral result. It cannot make us discover truths, enlighten us or prompt us to perform our duty. Aesthetic culture would rather leave man entirely indeterminate to do what he will (Twenty-first Letter):

> But in just this way something infinite is achieved. For as soon as we recall that this liberty was taken from him by the unilateral compulsion of nature in the realm of sensation, and the exclusive legislation of reason in the realm of thought, then we have to admit that the capacity which the aesthetic disposition restores to him is the highest of all bounties: the bounty of humanity.

Thus only through this (temporary) condition of aesthetic freedom or indeterminism can we realize the full capacity of our being. Equally, beauty is not only a symbol of this equilibrium. Human self-realization or wholeness is itself a form of beauty which allows us to fully articulate our moral autonomy.

We have now come full circle. Individual harmonization through aesthetic experience, allowing for the development of moral freedom and for a reunification of our human faculties, creates a sociable character which, according to Schiller, leads to a further harmonization of social relations in society. Aesthetic education, he argues, helps to overcome the moral state of nature of egoist antagonism threatening the fundaments of the existing society and preventing a transition to the *Vernunftstaat*. Strikingly, Schiller takes no recourse to a model of strong sociability. Aesthetic education does not bring about communitarian patriotism or the brotherly love of *fraternité*. By contrast, he links aesthetic sociability with the loose sociability of taste and courtly politeness. Schiller here freely follows Kant's claim that our pleasure in beauty is inseparably linked to its communicability. But Schiller turns Kant's meaning on its head. Taste does not merely build on our sociable drives but itself becomes a central vehicle of socialization. Instead of strong social bonds, Schiller suggests, modern society could rest on something like the shared but modest and detached joys displayed by a group of art connoisseurs. The hard-won faculty of taste, not joint political values or religious beliefs, here becomes the vehicle for achieving social consensus and judgements coordinated in a peaceful way. In eighteenth-century thought, this outcome was termed common sense.

To be sure, *On the Aesthetic Education of Man* is anything but a rounded academic tract on aesthetics and politics, leaving as it does many questions unanswered. How exactly would aesthetic education be implemented? What is the relation between the harmony-based model of liquifying beauty and the dynamic model of energetic beauty? But it must be remembered that the text is basically a fragment, a part of a larger, unfinished project. It shares this fate with some of the most important works in eighteenth-century thought, such as Rousseau's *Social Contract*.

When the Council of Europe in 1972 made Schiller's 1785 'Ode to Joy' in Beethoven's beautiful 1824 setting the anthem of the European Community (now the European Union), it adopted not only a drinking song but also Schiller's early vision of a cosmic fraternal sociability of all men as its official hymn. Now, as this and other political projects face colossal practical challenges of coordination, (dis-)integration and transition, it might be a fitting moment to look again at Schiller's much cooler, later vision of how to achieve freedom and consensus in modern society through the cultivation of our feelings and judgements.

NOTES

1. Terry Eagleton, *The Ideology of the Aesthetic* (Oxford: Blackwell, 1990), pp. 102–22; Jürgen Habermas, *The Philosophical Discourse of Modernity: Twelve Lectures*, trans. Frederick Lawrence (Cambridge, MA: MIT Press, 1987), pp. 45–50; Lesley Sharpe, *Schiller's Aesthetic Essays: Two Centuries of Criticism* (Columbia, SC: Camden House, 1995); Georg Bollenbeck, *Eine Geschichte der Kulturkritik. Von Rousseau bis Günther Anders* (Munich: C. H. Beck, 2007), pp. 76–110.

2. NA 27, p. 125; NA 27, p. 92. Quotations from *On the Aesthetic Education of Man* and the *Letters* to Augustenburg are taken from Keith Tribe's translations herein. All others are my own, unless otherwise stated.

3. NA 20, pp. 92f.

4. NA 20.1, pp. 37–75.

5. On this complex see Hans-Jürgen Schings, *Die Brüder des Marquis Posa: Schiller und der Geheimbund der Illuminaten* (Tübingen: Niemeyer, 1996), esp. ch. 8.

6. Quoted after Hans Schulz, *Friedrich Christian, Herzog zu Schleswig-Holstein: Ein Lebenslauf* (Stuttgart and Leipzig: Deutsche Verlags-Anstalt, 1910), p. 68.

7. Quoted after Schings, *Die Brüder des Marquis Posa*, pp. 201–2.

8. *Timoleon und Immanuel. Dokumente einer Freundschaft. Briefwechsel zwischen Friedrich Christian von Schleswig-Holstein und Jens Baggesen*, ed. Hans Schulz (Leipzig: S. Hirzel, 1910), pp. 157 and 161.

9. NA 22, pp. 106–9.

10. See Alexander Schmidt, 'Freedom and State Action in German Late Enlightenment Thought', in *Freedom and the Construction of Europe*, ed. Quentin Skinner and Martin van Gelderen, vol. 2 (Cambridge: Cambridge University Press, 2013), pp. 208–26.

11. Karl Leonhard Reinhold, 'Die drey Stände. Ein Dialog', *Der neue Teutsche Merkur* (1792), 1, pp. 217–41, quote p. 218.

12. Henri Grégoire, 'Fortgesetzter Bericht über den Zustand der schönen Künste im neuen Frankreich', trans. Karl August Böttiger, *Der neue Teutsche Merkur* (1795), 1, pp. 169–70.

13. NA 26, pp. 298–9.

14. AA 8, p. 366.

15. Patrick Riley, *Will and Political Legitimacy: A Critical Exposition of Social Contract Theory in Hobbes, Locke, Rousseau, Kant, and Hegel* (Cambridge, MA, and London: Harvard University Press, 1982), p. 15.

16. See Alexander Schmidt, 'The Liberty of the Ancients? Friedrich Schiller and Aesthetic Republicanism', *History of Political Thought,* 30 (2009), pp. 286–314.

17. NA 19.1, p. 16.

18. Riley, *Will and Political Legitimacy,* p. 203.

19. David Hume, 'Enquiry concerning Human Understanding', in *Enquiries concerning Human Understanding and concerning the Principles of Morals,* ed. L. A. Selby-Bigge, 3rd edn revised by P. H. Nidditch (Oxford: Clarendon Press, 1975), p. 298.

20. Immanuel Kant, *Critique of the Power of Judgment,* trans. Paul Guyer and Eric Matthews (Cambridge: Cambridge University Press, 2000), p. 225 (§59).

21. Michael Sonenscher, *Sans-Culottes: An Eighteenth-Century Emblem in the French Revolution* (Princeton and Oxford: Princeton University Press, 2008), p. 26.

22. Johann Georg Sulzer, *Allgemeine Theorie der schönen Künste in einzeln, nach alphabetischer Ordnung der Kunstwörter auf einander folgenden Artikeln,* 2nd edn, vol. 1 (Leipzig: Weidmannschen Buchhandlung, 1792 [1771–4]), p. xiii.

23. Henry Home, Lord Kames, *Elements of Criticism,* ed. and with an introduction by Peter Jones (Indianapolis: Liberty Fund, 2005), p. 724 (ch. 25).

24. Ibid., pp. 3–4.

25. Adam Smith, *An Inquiry into the Nature and Causes of the Wealth of Nations,* 2 vols, ed. R. H. Campbell, A. S. Skinner and W. B. Todd (Oxford: Oxford University Press, 1976), p. 796 (V, i, g, 15).

26. NA 20, p. 134.

27. On this complex see Eva Piirimäe and Alexander Schmidt, 'Introduction: Between Morality and Anthropology – Sociability in Enlightenment Thought', *History of European Ideas,* 41 (2015), pp. 571–88.

28. See Sabine Roehr, 'Freedom and Autonomy in Schiller', *Journal of the History of Ideas,* 64 (2003), pp. 119–34.

29. Karl Leonhard Reinhold, *Briefe über die Kantische Philosophie,* vol. 2 (Leipzig: Georg Joachim Göschen, 1792), esp. p. 182.

30. Frederick Beiser, *Schiller as Philosopher: A Re-examination* (Oxford and New York: Oxford University Press, 2005), pp. 150–64.

Further Reading

The overwhelming majority of the research literature on Schiller's *On the Aesthetic Education of Man* is in German. A comprehensive account is given in Carsten Zelle's excellent entry on *Über die ästhetische Erziehung des Menschen* in the *Schiller-Handbuch* (2005). The following small selection brings together some essential readings from recent German, French and Anglophone scholarship.

SCHILLER'S LIFE AND WORK

Alt, Peter-André, *Schiller. Leben-Werk-Zeit. Eine Biographie*, 2 vols., 2nd edn (Munich: C. H. Beck, 2004).

Reed, Terence James, *Schiller* (Oxford and New York: Oxford University Press, 1991).

EDITIONS OF SCHILLER'S THEORETICAL WRITINGS

On the Aesthetic Education of Man, in a Series of Letters, ed. and trans. Elizabeth M. Wilkinson and L. A. Willoughby (Oxford: Clarendon Press, 1967).

Dewhurst, Kenneth and Nigel Reeves, *Friedrich Schiller: Medicine, Psychology and Literature: With the First English Edition of His Complete Medical and Psychological Writings* (Berkeley: University of California Press, 1978).

On the Naive and Sentimental in Literature, ed. and trans. Helen Watanabe-O'Kelly (Manchester: Carcanet New Press, 1981).

Werke und Briefe in zwölf Bänden, vol. 8: *Theoretische Schriften*, ed. Rolf-Peter Janz et al. (Frankfurt am Main: Deutscher Klassiker Verlag, 1992).

Essays, ed. Walter Hinderer and Daniel O. Dahlstrom (New York: Continuum, 1993).

Curran, Jane V., Christophe Fricker et al., *Schiller's 'On Grace and Dignity' in Its Cultural Context: Essays and a New Translation* (Rochester, NY: Camden House, 2005).

Über die ästhetische Erziehung des Menschen, in Einer Reihe von Briefen, ed. and commentary Stefan Matuschek (Frankfurt am Main: Suhrkamp, 2009).

CRITICISM AND COMMENTARY

Agard, Olivier and Françoise Lartillot (eds.), *L'éducation esthétique selon Schiller: Entre anthropologie, politique et théorie du beau* (Paris: L'Harmattan, 2013).

Beiser, Frederick, *Schiller as Philosopher: A Re-examination* (Oxford and New York: Oxford University Press, 2005).

Beiser, Frederick, '*Schiller as Philosopher*: A Reply to My Critics', *Inquiry* 51 (2008), pp. 63–78.

Guyer, Paul, *Kant and the Experience of Freedom: Essays on Aesthetics and Morality* (Cambridge: Cambridge University Press, 1996).

Henrich, Dieter, 'Beauty and Freedom: Schiller's Struggle with Kant's Aesthetics', in *Essays in Kant's Aesthetics*, ed. Ted Cohen and Paul Guyer (Chicago and London: University of Chicago Press, 1982), pp. 237–57.

Hinderer, Walter, 'Schiller's Philosophical Aesthetics in Anthropological Perspective', in *A Companion to the Works of Friedrich Schiller*, ed. Steven D. Martinson (Rochester, NY: Camden House, 2005), pp. 27–46.

Martinson, Steven D., *Harmonious Tensions: The Writings of Friedrich Schiller* (Newark and London: University of Delaware Press, 1996).

Moggach, Douglas, 'Aesthetics and Politics', in *The Cambridge History of Nineteenth-century Political Thought*, ed. Gareth Stedman Jones and Gregory Claeys (Cambridge: Cambridge University Press, 2011), pp. 479–520.

Pugh, David, *Dialectic of Love: Platonism in Schiller's Aesthetics* (Montreal: McGill-Queen's University Press, 1996).

Riedel, Wolfgang, *Die Anthropologie des jungen Schiller* (Würzburg: Königshausen und Neumann, 1985).

Roehr, Sabine, 'Freedom and Autonomy in Schiller', *Journal of the History of Ideas*, 64 (2003), pp. 119–34.

Savile, Anthony, *Aesthetic Reconstructions: The Seminal Writings of Lessing, Kant and Schiller* (Oxford and New York: Blackwell, 1987).

Schmidt, Alexander, 'The Liberty of the Ancients? Friedrich Schiller and Aesthetic Republicanism', *History of Political Thought*, 30 (2009), pp. 286–314.

Schmidt, Alexander, 'Freedom and State Action in German Late Enlightenment Thought', in *Freedom and the Construction of Europe*, ed. Quentin Skinner and Martin van Gelderen, vol. 2 (Cambridge: Cambridge University Press, 2013), pp. 208–26.

Sharpe, Lesley, *Friedrich Schiller: Drama, Thought and Politics* (Cambridge: Cambridge University Press, 1991).

Sharpe, Lesley, *Schiller's Aesthetic Essays: Two Centuries of Criticism* (Columbia, SC: Camden House, 1995).

Sharpe, Lesley, 'Concerning Aesthetic Education', in *A Companion to the Works of Friedrich Schiller*, ed. Steven D. Martinson (Rochester, NY: Camden House, 2005), pp. 147–67.

Zelle, Carsten, '*Über die ästhetische Erziehung des Menschen in einer Reihe von Briefen*', in *Schiller-Handbuch*, ed. Matthias Luserke-Jaqui (Stuttgart and Weimar: Metzler, 2005), pp. 409–45.

Abbreviations

AA (Akademie-Ausgabe): Immanuel Kant, *Gesammelte Schriften*, ed. Preußische Akademie der Wissenschaften, 29 vols. (Berlin: G. Reimer, 1900–).

NA ([Schiller] Nationalausgabe): Friedrich Schiller, *Werke*, ed. Goethe- und Schiller-Archiv, Schiller-Nationalmuseum and Deutsche Akademie (Weimar: H. Böhlau, 1943–).

Note on the Text

The translation of *On the Aesthetic Education of Man, in a Series of Letters* is based on the first edition published in the journal *Die Horen* (1795), first issue, pp. 7–48 (First to Ninth Letters), 2nd issue, pp. 51–94 (Tenth to Sixteenth Letters) and 6th issue, pp. 45–124 (Seventeenth to Twenty-seventh Letters). To improve readability we have dropped the subheadings, which in *Die Horen* merely indicated a continuation from the previous letters. The German text is printed in Friedrich Schiller, *Werke und Briefe in zwölf Bänden*, vol. 8: *Theoretische Schriften*, ed. Rolf-Peter Janz et al. (Frankfurt am Main: Deutscher Klassiker Verlag, 1992), pp. 556–676. A digital version of this journal can now be accessed via the website of the Retrospektive Digitalisierung project of the Universitätsbibliothek of Bielefeld: http://www.ub.uni-bielefeld.de/diglib/aufklaerung (last accessed 2 February 2016). The original title is *Ueber die ästhetische Erziehung des Menschen, in einer Reyhe von Briefen*. Schiller made several changes for the second edition in 1801 as part of his collected prose writings (*Kleinere prosaische Schriften*, vol. 3 (Leipzig: Crusius, 1801), pp. 44–309). These changes included a shortening of footnotes and of the subheadings. The last footnote (p. 112) was drawn into the main body of the text and its last two sentences cut in order to conceal the unfinished character of the text. Responding to the intervention of his friend Christian Gottfried Körner, Schiller also changed *Sachtrieb* (material impulse) into *Stofftrieb*.

The translation of the letters to Augustenburg is based on the German original published in the *Nationalausgabe: Schillers Werke*, vol. 26: *Briefwechsel: Schillers Briefe 1.3.1790–17.5.1794,* ed. Edith Nahler and Horst Nahler (Weimar: Hermann Böhlaus Nachfolger, 1992), pp. 183; 257–268; 295–333; 337–338 (nrs. 152, 184, 208, 209, 210, 213). They were first published together in *Deutsche Rundschau*, vol. 7, in 1876. With slight changes Schiller published the letter of 3 December 1793 under the title *Ueber den moralischen Nutzen ästhetischer Sitten* (*On the Moral Use of Aesthetic Manners*) in the first issue of *Die Horen* in 1796.

We are painfully aware that the English language does not offer a fully satisfying equivalent term to the German *Mensch* that is both gender-neutral and stylistically sound. Throughout the text 'man' and its respective pronouns and possessives are thus used in a gender-neutral sense.

ON THE AESTHETIC
EDUCATION OF MAN
IN A SERIES OF LETTERS*

---

* These letters have really been written; but to *whom* is here of no relevance, and will perhaps in time be made known to the reader. As letters, however, they retain little more than their division into a sequence, since it was considered necessary to suppress everything of local connection, without wanting to put anything in its place; which would have been an impropriety easily avoided if one had been less concerned about their authenticity.

ON THE AESTHETIC
EDUCATION OF MAN

If it is reason that makes man, it is sentiment that guides
him.

Rousseau[1]

FIRST LETTER

So you would like me to give you the results of my investigations *into beauty and art* as a series of letters. I can sense the
real gravity, but also the attraction and distinction, of such an
enterprise. I will talk of something directly connected with the
greater part of our happiness, and something that is not unre-
lated to the moral nobility of human nature. My presentation
of beauty will often need to invoke feelings as well as principles; but the heart which I address does sense the great power
of beauty, and acts upon it, relieving me of the most difficult
part of my labour.

What I had intended to ask of you as a favour you have
generously made a duty, leaving me the appearance of merit
when I am merely following my own inclination. The freedom
of approach that you prescribe is no constraint, more my own
need. I am little used to the ways of formal scholarship, so I
will hardly be in danger of offending good taste by their abuse.
My ideas have been formed more in continual communion
with myself than from extensive worldly experience, or reading; they will be unable to deny their origin, will be guilty of
any kind of error but that of sectarianism, will fail more from
their own weakness than stand by virtue of authority and a
strength they do not themselves possess.

I will not conceal from you that the following assertions will
for the most part rest on Kantian principles; but please blame
my own inability, and not these principles, if in what follows
you should be reminded of any particular philosophical school.
No, for me the freedom of your mind must remain inviolate.
Your own feeling will give me the facts upon which I build,

your own independent powers of thought will dictate the laws of procedure to which we must adhere.

Only philosophers are divided about the ruling ideas in the practical part of the Kantian system,[1] while I trust I can prove that men and women have always been at one on them. One must only detach these ideas from their technical form for them to stand revealed as primordial statements of common sense, and as facts of the moral instinct which wise nature lent man until such time as clear insight emancipates him from such tutelage. However, while this technical form reveals truth to our understanding, it also conceals truth from our feeling; because, unfortunately, understanding has first to destroy the object of inner reflection if it would really make this object its *own*. Just like the chemist, the philosopher can discover connection only through dissolution, only through the rigours of artifice discover the work of a free nature. To catch hold of fleeting appearance he must shackle it with rules, tear into its fair body with concepts, and preserve its living spirit in a meagre frame of words. Is it any wonder if natural feeling can no longer be found in such an image, and that in the hands of the analyst truth seems to be paradoxical?

So please bear with me if, in the course of the following studies, my approach to an understanding of our object moves it beyond reach of our senses. What has been said of moral experience is even more true for the phenomenon we call beauty. Its entire magic rests upon its secret, and by dissolving the necessary bond between its elements its very being melts away.

SECOND LETTER

But should I not make better use of the liberty you have allowed me, rather than directing your attention to the domain of the fine arts? Is it not somewhat untimely to seek a code of law for the aesthetic world, while the affairs of the moral world raise matters of much more direct interest, and the spirit of philosophical inquiry is expressly challenged by the present circumstances to address the most perfect of all works of art: the construction of a true political liberty?

I would not wish to live in any different century, nor to have worked for any other. We are just as much citizens of our time as we are citizens of our state; and if it appears unseemly, even impermissible, to exempt oneself from the morals and customs of the milieu in which one lives, why should it be any less a duty to allow the needs and tastes of this century a voice in choosing what one does?

But this voice does not seem to favour art; at least not the kind of art to which my study will be devoted. The course of events has lent the spirit of the age a direction that threatens to render the art of the ideal ever more remote from this spirit. This art has to leave the realm of reality, and with proper audacity elevate itself above simple need; for art is a daughter of freedom, responding not to the demands of matter, but to the necessity in our minds. For the present, need prevails, and bends a sunken humanity to its tyrannical yoke. *Utility* is the great idol of the age, to which all powers are in thrall and all talent must pay homage. On this crude scale the spiritual virtues of art have no weight and, bereft of all encouragement, it disappears from the tumultuous market of our century. The spirit of philosophical inquiry strips the power of imagination from one province after another; the borders of art shrink as science extends its bounds.

The gaze of both philosopher and man of the world is now fixed expectantly on the political domain, where the very fate of humanity is argued out; or so it is thought. Does not any failure to join with this argument betray a culpable indifference to the welfare of society? However important the substance and consequence of this great legal dispute might be to anyone calling himself a man, the way in which it is conducted should be of especial interest to anyone who can think for himself. A question that would otherwise be settled by the blind right of might now seems to have been brought before the tribunal of pure reason; and whoever remains capable of putting himself at the centre of things, advancing from a mere individual to a representative of the human race, might equally consider himself a member of this tribunal, as he is, as human being and citizen of the world, party at the same time and more or less caught up in its outcome. It is hence not just his own interests that will be decided by this legal process; judgment will also be made according to laws which his rational mind is competent and entitled to dictate.

How inspiring it would be for me to address such things in company with someone who is as witty a thinker as he is a liberal citizen of the world, leaving any decision to a heart so keenly devoted to the welfare of mankind! How pleasantly surprising it would be, given all difference in station and in the great distance imposed by worldly circumstance, to find agreement in the field of ideas with a mind as unprejudiced as yours! That I resist such an alluring temptation and put beauty before liberty can, I think, be justified not only by my own inclination, but also by principles. I hope to convince you that this matter is far less alien to the needs of the age than it is to its taste; and that if one is to resolve this political problem one must in practice take the aesthetic path, for it is by way of beauty that one approaches liberty. This proof cannot be made, however, without my reminding you of the principles by which the exercise of reason is guided in the work of political legislation.

THIRD LETTER

Nature treats man no better than the rest of it works: it acts for him whenever he, as a free and spontaneous agent, is not yet able to act. This is what makes him a man: that he does not settle for what nature made of him, but has the ability to re-enact by means of reason those steps it has taken on his behalf, transforming a work born of need into one of his own free choice, elevating physical necessity to a moral necessity.

He gains consciousness from sensuous slumber, sees that he is a man, looks around and finds himself to be living in a state. Force of need cast him there before he was capable of freely choosing this condition; and need arranged the state, according to purely natural laws before *he* was able to do so, making use of the laws of reason. But as a moral person he neither could nor can be satisfied with a provisional state, which was prompted merely by his natural determination, and was intended to serve it alone – and it would be all the worse for him if he were content with this condition! By the same right that makes him a man he thus abandons the rule of blind necessity, parting from it, as in so many other matters, through his freedom; just as, taking only one example, he suppresses through morality, and refines through beauty, the coarse character that the need of sexual love expressed. And so, through artifice, he retrieves his childhood, imagining a *state of nature* as an idea that no experience has given him, but which has been imposed by his determination as a reasoning being. And in this ideal condition he adopts a purpose not known in his real natural state, a choice of which he was not then capable, now proceeding in no other way than as if he were beginning all over again, as if he had, purely of his own clear insight and free volition, exchanged the condition of independence for one of contract. However skilfully and solidly blind caprice does its work, with what presumption that which it has once created is sustained, in whatever semblance of reverence it might clothe itself – man can nonetheless regard it as something that never happened; for the work of blind caprice has no authority before which liberty must bend, everything has to find its place in the supreme purpose that reason now demands of him as a person. This is the origin and justification of the attempt by an emancipated people to re-form its natural state into a moral order.

This natural state (as any political body that derives its original existence from forces and not from laws can be called) does stand in contradiction to moral man, for whom the only law should be to act in conformity with the law; but it is sufficient for physical man, who gives himself laws only so that he might come to terms with forces. However, physical man *actually* exists, while moral man is merely *a problem yet to be solved*. Once reason abolishes the natural state, as it must necessarily do if it is to assume its place, it risks physical, actual man for the sake of a moral man as yet unformed, risks the existence of society for a merely potential ideal society (if also a morally necessary one). Reason takes from man something that he really possesses, and without which he would have nothing, pointing him towards something that he could, and should, possess; and if this turns out to be asking too much of him reason would, for the sake of a humanity that he still lacks, a lack that does his existence no harm, tear him from that animal existence which is actually the condition of his humanity. Before man had time to align his will with the law, reason would have snatched the ladder of nature out from under his feet.

The great problem is that physical society cannot cease to exist for a moment *in time* while moral society is forming *as an idea*; that man's sheer existence cannot be endangered for the sake of his moral dignity. When a craftsman repairs a timepiece he can still its wheels; but the living clockwork of the state has to be repaired while it continues to strike, the turning wheel has to be replaced while still in motion. Support has to be found to secure the continuation of society, rendering it independent of the natural state that one seeks to transcend.

This support cannot be found in the natural character of man, for this character is selfish and violent, more inclined to the destruction of society than to its preservation. Nor can it be found in his moral character, for, as we have seen, this must first be cultivated; and the legislator could never act, nor ever depend with any degree of certainty upon this character, because it is free and *never made manifest*. One must therefore part licence from man's physical character, and freedom from his moral character, bringing the first into conformity with law and making the second dependent upon sense-impressions. This would remove the former rather further from matter, while bringing the latter somewhat closer, so that a third character might be created which, related to both, could create a path from the rule of naked force to the rule of laws; and which, without hindering the development of moral character, served instead as a sensible pledge of an invisible morality.

FOURTH LETTER

This much is certain: only a preponderance of this kind of character among a people can render harmless the transformation of a state according to moral principles, and only this character can secure its persistence. The formation of a moral state will require that the moral order be a motivating force; free will is to be drawn into the causal domain in which everything is connected with strict necessity and constancy. However, we know that the human will is ruled by contingency, and that only in the Supreme Being do physical and moral necessity coincide. If then we are to count on man's moral conduct with as much certainty as we count upon *natural* events, then this conduct must *be* his nature, and he must be led by these impulses to conduct which is always of a moral character. Human will has a completely free choice between duty and inclination, and this sovereign right of his person can and should be infringed by no physical compulsion. If he is to retain this capacity to choose, while remaining all the same a dependable link in the causal connection of powers, this can happen only if the effects of both duty and inclination are indistinguishable in the empire of appearances; and, for all the difference of form, the content of his volition remains the same – that therefore his impulses coincide sufficiently with his reason for universal legislation to be possible.

It can be said that every individual carries within himself, by disposition and vocation, a purely ideal man, the great task of his existence being to reconcile all his shifts and changes with its immutable unity.*[1] This pure man, visible more or less clearly in every subject, is represented by the state: the objective and also canonical form in which the diversity of subjects seeks unity.[2] Now there are two distinct ways in which we might imagine how temporal man coincides with the idea of man, and just as many ways in which the state can manifest itself in individuals: either through the pure man suppressing empirical man (the state suppressing individuality), or by the individual *becoming* the state (temporal man *refining* himself into the idea of man).

In a unilateral moral evaluation this difference collapses, for reason is satisfied as long as its laws are unconditionally observed. But in entirely anthropological terms, where both form and content are of importance and living sensation also has a voice, this difference becomes all the more important. Reason furthers unity, but nature furthers diversity; both lay claim to man. The law of reason is imprinted upon him by an incorruptible consciousness, the law of nature by an ineradicable feeling. It will be proof of a deficiency of upbringing if moral character can prevail only by sacrificing the natural; and the constitution of a state will be very incomplete if it can bring about unity only by suppressing diversity. The state should honour in individuals not only the objective and generic but also their subjective and specific character, and ensure that, in extending the invisible empire of morals, the empire of appearance is not depleted.

When the mechanic artisan takes up a shapeless mass to form it for his own ends, he has no reservations about applying force; for the natural material with which he works deserves in itself no consideration, and his concern is not with the whole for the sake of its parts, but with the parts for the sake of the whole. When the artist takes up the same mass, he likewise has little concern about applying force; he wishes only to avoid showing that he does so. He has no more respect for

* I refer here to a text by my friend Fichte which has recently been published, *Lectures on the Vocation of the Scholar*, in which he illuminates this principle in a manner never before attempted.

the material with which he works than does the mechanic artisan, but he will seek through apparent pliancy to deceive the
eye which guards the liberty of this material. It is completely
different with educational and political craftsmen, for whom
the human being is both material and object of attention. Here
purpose becomes material again, and only because the whole
serves the parts might the parts align themselves with the whole.
The state craftsman must have a consideration for his material
quite different from that to which the artist pretends; he must
respect its uniqueness and personality not merely subjectively,
seeking an illusory impact upon the senses, but objectively,
directed to its inner being.

But since the state should be an organization that creates
itself for itself, it can only be realized if the parts have been
attuned to the idea of the whole. Because the state represents
the pure and objective humanity in the hearts of its citizens,
it will have to observe with respect to its citizens the same
relationship as each has to himself, and will be able to honour their subjective humanity only to the extent that it is
refined into objective humanity. If the inner man is at one
with himself he will preserve his individuality even when his
conduct is subject to the greatest universalization, and the
state will simply become the expositor of his finest instinct,
the clearer formulation of his inner sense of right. If, on the
other hand, subjective man is set against objective man in
the character of a people in such a way that the latter can
win out only by suppressing the former, the state will then
impose the full rigour of the law on its citizens and, so as not
to become their victim, trample upon inimical individuality
regardless.

However, man can be at odds with himself in two ways:
either as a savage, his feelings ruling his principles; or as a barbarian, if his principles destroy his feelings. The savage despises
artifice, recognizing nature as his unlimited domain; the barbarian scorns and dishonours nature; but more contemptibly
than the savage, he often enough continues to be the slave of
his slave. The cultured man makes nature his friend, honouring
its freedom by taming only its caprice.

If, therefore, reason introduces moral unity to physical society, it must not harm the diversity of nature. If nature seeks to maintain diversity in the moral construction of society, this must not infringe moral unity; the triumph of form is equidistant from uniformity on the one hand and confusion on the other. A *totality* of character has therefore to be found in the people both capable and worthy of exchanging the state of compulsion for that of liberty.

FIFTH LETTER

Is it this character – that of our present age – that current events show us? I turn straight away to the most prominent object in this vast canvas.

It is true that the standing of opinion has fallen, arbitrary rule has been unmasked and, while still armed with power, it can no longer lay any claim to honour. Man has at last awoken from indolence and self-deception, and with an emphatic majority demands to be restored into his inalienable rights. But man does not only make demands; on both sides of the Atlantic he is rising up to take by force what he thinks has been unlawfully denied him. The fabric of the natural state is tottering, its rotting foundations give way and there seems to be the *physical* possibility of enthroning the law, of finally treating man as an end in himself, and making true liberty the foundation of political association. Vain hope! The *moral* possibility is lacking, and a moment of such possibility finds itself confronted with an unreceptive generation.

Man portrays himself by his deeds, and what kind of image is shaped in the drama of the present! Here a relapse into savagery, there lethargy: the two extremes of human degradation, united in one single epoch.

We observe rough and licentious instincts among the lower and more numerous classes, which, after the dissolution of civil order, hurry with ungovernable fury to their animal gratification. It may therefore be that objective mankind had reason for complaint with the state; nonetheless, subjective mankind has to honour its institutions. Can one blame the state for disregarding the dignity of human nature, so long as its very existence had to be defended? That it hastened to divide by force of gravity, and bind through force of cohesion, when it was not yet time to think of organic development? Its dissolution was its own justification. Society, loosened of all control, falls back into an elemental domain, instead of hurrying upwards into an organic life.

On the other hand, the civilized classes present the even more repugnant spectacle of lethargy and a depraved character which is all the more disgusting because culture itself is its source. I no longer recall which of the old or new philosophers remarked that the more refined a thing, the more repulsive its decay; but this is also true of the moral sphere. If the child of nature breaks loose, he becomes a madman; the pupil of art, despicable. The enlightenment of understanding that the finer ranks not unjustly praise has on the whole had so little refining influence on resolve that it has instead tended to reinforce corruption through principle. We disown nature in its proper domain only to experience its tyranny in the moral sphere, and while we resist the impression nature makes upon us, we adopt its principles as our own. The pretended decency of our manners refuses nature the *first* (pardonable) word, only to give it, in our materialist moral philosophy, the decisive *last* word. Egoism has established its system at the heart of the most elaborated sociability, and in the absence of its very own sociable heart we experience all the contagion and affliction of society. We subordinate our free judgement to the despotic opinion of society, our feeling to its bizarre customs, our will to its seductions – it is only our impulsiveness that we maintain in the face of its divine laws. A complacent egoism seizes the heart of the man of the world, a heart that in the primitive natural man often beats in sympathy, and each seeks to save just himself, as those fleeing a burning town seek to rescue their meagre property from destruction. It is thought that only by completely abjuring sensibility can we find protection against its aberrations, and the ridicule that often serves to chasten and rein in the enthusiast is directed with equal disregard to the most refined feeling. Culture, far from setting us free, develops in every capacity with which we are cultivated merely a new need; physical bonds lace themselves ever tighter around us, such that our fear of losing what we have extinguishes even the fiery impulse for improvement, and the maxim of passive obedience is taken for supreme wisdom. The spirit of the age thus vacillates between perversity and brutality, between unnatural and bare nature, between superstition and moral unbelief, and it is only the balance of evil that sets a temporary limit.

SIXTH LETTER

Does this image of the age really go too far? I do not expect this objection to be made; rather another, that I have in this way proved too much. You will tell me that this image does resemble contemporary mankind, but it also resembles all cultured peoples, since all of them, without exception, must be led away from nature by sophistry before they can return to nature through reason.

Yet closer attention to the character of the age will make us wonder about the contrast between the form taken by mankind today and that of earlier forms, especially that of the Greeks.[1] Our reputation for education and refinement, which we rightly value by comparison with all other *merely* natural humanity, is pulled up short by the natural humanity of the Greeks, for they freely embraced all the delights of art and worthiness of wisdom, though without being seduced by them as we have been. The Greeks not only shame us by a simplicity that is alien to our age; they are also our rivals, even our models, in respect of those very advantages in which we seek consolation and reassurance for our unnatural manners. At once complete in form and substance, at once philosophical and creative, at once gentle and energetic, the Greeks united the youth of imagination with the manhood of reason in a glorious humanity.

At that beautiful time of the awakening of spiritual powers, sense and spirit had as yet no clearly separate domains; there had been no dissent that might have prompted them to form hostile, strictly demarcated camps. Poetry had not yet wooed wit, speculation had not yet ruined itself through sophistry. If need be they could exchange functions, for each honoured truth in its own way. However high the flight of reason, it made sure to retain its substance; however finely and sharply it made distinctions, it cut no corners. It did pull human nature apart and projected each element, enlarged, into the wonderful world of its gods; although this human nature was not merely broken into fragments, but combined in different proportions, no single deity lacking humanity in its entirety. How different are we moderns! The image of the human species in each of us has been enlarged, shattered and scattered as shards, not in proportioned admixtures; so that one has to go from one individual to another to reconstitute the totality of the species. One might almost say that in practice our faculties express themselves as fragments corresponding to the analytical distinctions of the psychologist; not only individual subjects but entire classes of men realize only one part of their endowments, while the remainder remain stunted, leaving hardly a dull trace of themselves.

I am not overlooking the advantages that the human race today enjoys with respect to the best of their predecessors, taken as a whole and weighed on the scales of understanding; but in any such contest like must be measured in turn against like. Which modern man is prepared to challenge any one Athenian to debate the prize of humanity?

Why should individuals be so disadvantaged, given all the advantages of the species? How did an individual Greek come to be representative of his era, and why does no modern man claim this distinction? Because the first was formed as a unity by nature, and the second by an intellect that divided and subdivided.

It was culture itself that wounded modern humanity in this way. On the one hand, the extension of empirical knowledge and sharper thinking rendered a more precise distinction of the sciences necessary, while on the other the elaborate machinery of the state demanded a more consistent separation of ranks and occupations; the inner unity of human nature was torn apart, and a ruinous dispute set its harmonious powers at odds. Intuitive and speculative understanding became inimical and occupied their own domains, whose border they now began to patrol with jealous mistrust; and the spheres within which their activities were confined were now ruled by a master they had themselves chosen, who not infrequently sought to suppress as inessential all other human endowments. While here an excessive imagination laid waste to the hard-won fruits of understanding, elsewhere the spirit of abstraction consumed the fire at which the heart should have warmed itself, and imagination been kindled.

The collapse which art and learning first brought about within man was made complete and universal by the new spirit of government. Of course, it was not to be expected that the simple organization of the first republics would survive the simplicity of initial manners and conditions, but instead of rising to a higher animalistic life, it descended into a crude and clumsy mechanism. Greek states resembled a colony of polyps,[2] for within them individuals enjoyed an independent life, although in time of necessity they could form into a whole; this now gave way to the artifice of a clockwork mechanism, the joining together of an infinite number of lifeless parts to create a new mechanically driven whole.[3] State and Church, laws and manners were now torn apart; pleasure was separated from work, means from end, effort from reward. Eternally shackled to one small fragment of the whole, man imagined himself to be a fragment, in his ear the constant and monotonous noise of the wheel that he turned; never capable of developing the harmony of his being, and instead of marking the humanity in his nature, he simply became the impress of his occupation, his particular knowledge.[4] But not even that bare fragmentary union still attaching the individual parts to the whole depended upon forms that they were able to determine themselves (for who would voluntarily surrender his liberty to a mechanism so artificial and shy of light?); any such autonomy was spurious, since the forms were in fact prescribed for them, inhibiting any free insight. Dead letters represent living intellect, a practised memory being a more reliable guide than genius and sensibility.

If the commonweal makes office the measure of the man, if it prizes in one citizen only his memory, in another only mathematical understanding, in a third only mechanical skill; if it is here indifferent to character and only interested in particular knowledge, but there by contrast a sense of order and lawful conduct is thought enough compensation for the most occult thinking – if at the same time these individual skills are to be pushed to such a degree of intensity as the subject allows in extension – should we be surprised that all other faculties of the mind are neglected, so that the one single faculty prized above all others should be exclusively rewarded? We do know that the powerful genius does not take the limits of his occupation to be the limits of his activity, but the mediocre talent uses up the entirety of his meagre powers in pursuing the occupation that has fallen to him; and anyone who has time left over for his own pursuits once his occupational duties are fulfilled must already be uncommonly gifted. Moreover, the state seldom thinks it any recommendation when powers exceed tasks; nor if the higher intellectual needs of the man of genius compete with the demands of office. The state jealously guards a monopoly over its servants; it would rather its man dallied with passions of the flesh than with those of the mind, and who could blame it for so doing?[5]

And, quite gradually, real individual life is extinguished, so that the threadbare existence of the abstract idea of the whole might prevail; the state remains for ever alien to its citizens, finding no feeling for it. Forced to deal with the diversity of its citizens through their classification, experiencing humanity only through representation, hence at second hand, the governor entirely loses contact with humanity, taking it for a mere construct of the intellect, while the governed are in turn indifferent to laws that barely relate to them. Wearying at last of maintaining a bond whose burden is so little eased by the state, positive society relapses into a moral state of nature – which has long been the fate of most European states; the public power becomes just *one party among many*, hated and circumvented by those for whom it exists, and recognized only by those who can do without it.

Faced with this dual force that presses upon it, both from within and from without, could humanity choose a path other than that which it actually took? Since the spirit of speculation in the world of ideas sought immemorial possessions, it had to become a stranger to the world of the senses, and through its concern with form lose sight of matter. Since practical spirit was locked into a monotonous world of objects, and there further restricted by formulation, the free whole receded from view, becoming likewise impoverished. Speculative spirit sought to model the real on the conceivable, exalting the subjective conditions of its powers of imagination into laws constitutive of the existence of things. By contrast, the practical spirit went to the opposite extreme, judging all experience whatsoever according to one particular fragment of that experience, seeking to impose without discrimination the rules governing *this* fragment upon each and every occupation. The first fell victim to empty subtlety, the second to a pedantic obtuseness; the former being too high-flown for the individual, the latter too unambitious to grasp the whole. The disadvantage of this last tendency was not merely limited to knowledge and production; it had no less an impact upon sensibility and action. We know that the degree of sensibility of the mind depends upon vivacity of imagination, its range upon imaginative powers. However, the preponderance of analytical power must necessarily rob the capacity for invention of both power and inspiration, a more restricted domain of objects reduce its wealth. Consequently, the abstract thinker very often has a *cold* heart, since he dissects the impressions that can touch his soul only in their entirety; the man of affairs very often has a *cramped* heart, because his power of imagination is confined to the uniform limits of his occupation, and is not capable of envisaging alien ways of thought.

I was minded to reveal the disadvantageous aspect of contemporary character and its sources, not to demonstrate the advantages with which nature endows it. I freely admit to you that, however little good this fragmentation of their being can do individuals, there is no other way in which the human species could have progressed. There is no doubt that the emergence of Greek humanity represented a maximum at which there could be neither pause nor further upward movement. There could be no pause, because intellect must have been inevitably compelled by knowledge already accumulated to separate itself from sensation and intuition in its striving for clarity of knowledge. There could be no further upward movement, because only a certain degree of clarity can coexist with a particular abundance and warmth. The Greeks had achieved this, and if they had wished to develop their culture further they would have had to surrender the totality of their being in the same way that we have had to, to pursue truth along separate lines.

There was no way of developing the various capacities of man other than to set them one against the another. The antagonism of powers is the great instrument of culture, but, all the same, only an instrument; for so long as this antagonism persists one is still on the path towards culture.[6] It is only because the individual powers of man separate themselves in this way, seeking exclusive authority, that they come into conflict with the truth of things and compel an idle common sense, that would not otherwise rise above external appearance, to penetrate to the heart of things. Since pure intellect usurps authority in the world of sense, while the empirical intellect seeks to subordinate pure intellect to the conditions of experience, both capacities develop to the greatest possible maturity, exhausting the full extent of their respective domains. Since the power of imagination also here dares dissolve the ordered world through its unconstrained freedom, it compels reason to become the supreme source of knowledge, calling upon the law of necessity for assistance in dealing with this capriciousness.

The unilateral exercise of powers does inevitably lead the individual into error, but it leads the species as a whole to truth. Solely by focussing the entire energy of our mind, and pulling our entire being together into one single power, we lend wings to this individual power, and through artifice lead it far beyond the limits that nature seems to have set it. Just as it is quite certain that all human individuals together, with the eyesight with which nature has endowed them, would never have discovered even one of the satellites of Jupiter revealed to the astronomer with the telescope, so it can also be agreed that human powers of thought would never have proposed an analysis of the infinite, nor a critique of pure reason, if the individuals so assembled had not isolated reason from everything material, readied their eyes and directed their attention to the absolute with the most intense abstraction. But will such a mind, dissolved into pure intellect and pure intuition, be suited to exchange the strict fetters of logic for the free course of poetic power, grasping hold of the individuality of things with true and chaste sense? Nature here sets even the universal genius a limit that he cannot cross, and truth will continue to make martyrs so long as philosophy has to make its prime concern the creation of safeguards against error.

However much the entire world might benefit from this separated development of human powers, it cannot be denied that the individuals involved are cursed by this universal purpose. While gymnastic exercise might create athletic bodies, beauty is created only by the free and regular play of the limbs. In the same way, harnessing together individual intellectual powers can certainly create extraordinary human beings, but only an equal intellectual temperament can make them happy and complete. And in what kind of relationship with former and future eras would we stand if the development of human nature made such a sacrifice necessary? We would have been the serfs of mankind, we would for a few thousand years have slaved for it, and our mutilated nature would be marked with the shameful traces of our servitude – so that a later generation might in blissful indolence maintain its moral health, and allow free rein to the development of its humanity!

But can man really be intended to neglect himself for the sake of any purpose? Should the purposes of nature rob us of a completeness which the purposes of reason prescribe for us? It must therefore be wrong that the development of individual powers requires the sacrifice of their totality; or if the rule of nature strives so for this end, then it is up to us to restore, through higher artifice, the totality in our nature that artifice has destroyed.

SEVENTH LETTER

Should we perhaps expect this to be done by the state? That is not possible, for the state in its present form has itself brought about the evil, and the state as conceived by reason would, instead of being able to establish this better humanity, have to be established upon this better humanity. This would have brought my studies right back to the point from which I had started, and from which my studies had for a time removed me. The present era is far from placing before us that form of humanity recognized to be the necessary condition for a moral reform of the state, and instead shows us something which is more like the direct opposite. If the principles I have advanced are correct, and if experience confirms my assessment of the present, then one has to declare that any attempt to bring about this kind of transformation in the state is untimely, and also declare any hope that might be founded upon this as chimerical, until such time as the inner separation of man is ended, and his nature is sufficiently developed to itself be the artist, and lend reality to the political creation of reason.

Nature shows us in its physical design the path we must take to moral existence. Not until the struggle of elemental forces in lower organisms has abated does nature begin with the noble formation of physical man. In the same way the elemental conflict within ethical man, the conflict of blind impulse, has to be stilled, and crude antagonism within him cease, before one might dare to favour diversity. On the other hand, the autonomy of his character has to be secured, and subordination to alien despotic forms give place to a respectable liberty, before the diversity in him might subordinate itself to the unity of the

ideal. Where natural man misuses so arbitrarily his voluntarism, here one might scarcely show him his liberty; where the
man of artifice still needs his liberty so little, one cannot here
take his voluntarism from him. The gift of liberal principles is
betrayal for the whole if it associates itself with a still ferment-
ing force, reinforcing a nature already overmighty; the rule of
conformity becomes tyranny against the individual if it associates itself with an already prevalent weakness and physical
limitation, extinguishing in this way the final flickers of autonomy and individuality.

The character of the age must therefore first lift itself from
its deep degradation, free itself of the blind force of nature to
which it was there subject and return to its simplicity, truth and
substance; a task that will take longer than a century. I freely
admit that some isolated efforts might succeed, but this will not
improve the whole, and the contradiction of conduct will constantly trump the unity of maxims. In other parts of the world
the humanity in the negro will be honoured,[1] while in Europe it
is disparaged in the thinker. The old principles will remain, but
clothed with the garb of the century, and philosophy will lend
its name to a repression formerly authorized by the Church.
Fearful of liberty, whose early efforts are always inimical, one
will either submit to an easy servitude or, brought to despair
by pedantic tutelage, escape to a state of nature lacking all constraint. Usurpation will invoke the weakness of human nature,
insurrection its dignity, until finally the great ruler of all human
affairs, blind might, intervenes, and decides what purports to
be a conflict of principles in the same way that it would a common brawl.

EIGHTH LETTER

Should therefore philosophy retire, discouraged and without hope, from this domain? While the rule of forms extends itself in every other direction should this, the most important of all possessions, be delivered up to faceless chance? Should the conflict of blind forces last an eternity in the political world, and the sociable law never vanquish hostile self-interest?

Not at all! Reason itself will not engage directly with a harsh power resistant to its weapons; no more than the son of Saturn in the *Iliad* will it stoop to take action in that grim arena.[1] Instead, reason chooses from among the ranks of warriors the most worthy, equips him like Zeus did his grandson with divine arms, and through his victorious power brings about the great decision.[2]

Reason has done what it can by discovering the law and establishing it; its execution is the task of resolute will and living feeling. If truth is to prevail in battle it must itself first become a *force*, establishing an *impelling force* as its champion in the realm of appearances; for impulses are the only motive forces in the sensible world. If reason has as yet showed little of its victorious power, this is not the fault of an intellect powerless to unveil it, but rather of the heart closed against it, and of the impulse that did not act in its favour.

So where does this still-prevailing rule of prejudice and smothering of minds come from, given the light shed by philosophy and experience? The era is enlightened, which means that knowledge has been discovered and made public sufficient to correct at least our practical principles. The spirit of free investigation has scattered those mistaken conceptions which have long barred the approach to truth, and has undermined the ground upon which fanaticism and deception had set their throne. Reason has cleansed itself from the deceptions of the senses and delusions of sophistry, and philosophy itself, which first made us disloyal to nature, now loudly and insistently calls us back into its arms – why, then, are we still barbarians?

Rather than in the things themselves, it must be something in men's psyche that obstructs the acceptance of truth, even when it burns so brightly, and the adoption of truth, even when it is so vividly convincing. A wise old man has sensed this, and it lies hidden in the pregnant statement: *sapere aude.*[3]

Have the courage to use your own understanding! The energy of courage needed to overcome the obstacles to learning thrown up by both the indolence of nature and the cowardice of the heart. Not for nothing does the ancient myth have the goddess of wisdom emerging fully armed from Jupiter's head;[4] for her very first action is that of a warrior. Even at her birth she must enter a bitter struggle with senses that do not wish to be torn from sweet repose. The more numerous part of mankind is too tired and exhausted from its struggle with need to gird itself up for a new and more intense struggle against error. Happy to avoid the troublesome effort of thinking, they gladly leave the control of their concepts to others; and if it so happens that they rouse themselves to higher needs, they seize with greedy credulity upon the formulations that state and priesthood have prepared for them in anticipation. If these unhappy souls deserve our sympathy, we are justified in despising those whom fortune has freed from the yoke of need, but who nonetheless choose to bend themselves to it. Such people prefer the twilight of obscure belief, in which one can feel more alive and shape the imagination in whatever way one likes, to the rays of truth that chase away the comforting delusions of their dreams. These illusions, which the malevolent light of knowledge threatens to scatter, are the basis of all their happiness; how can they be expected to pay so much for a truth that begins by robbing them of all they hold so dear? To love wisdom, they would already have to be wise, which itself is a truth already felt by those who gave philosophy its name.[5]

It is not therefore sufficient that all enlightenment of the intellect deserves recognition only insofar as it affects character; in part it derives from character, since the path to the head must be opened up through the heart. Culture of the capacity for feeling is the more urgent need at this time, not merely because it will enable better insight into life, but because it prompts the improvement of such insight itself.

NINTH LETTER

But have we not simply gone round in a circle? Theoretical culture should engender practical culture, while practical culture is still the condition of theoretical culture? All improvement in the domain of politics should derive from the refinement of character – but how can character be refined under the influence of a barbaric state order? One would need to find a tool suited to this task that the state does not possess, and with it open up sources that, for all political corruption, would remain pure and honest.

I have arrived at the point towards which all my previous observations have been moving: this tool is fine art; these sources open themselves up in its immortal examples.

Art, like science, is absolved from all that is positive and that human convention has introduced; both enjoy an absolute *immunity* from human capriciousness. The political legislator can bar the way to its domain, but he cannot rule within it. He can despise the friend of truth, but truth prevails; he can humiliate artists, but he cannot falsify art. Of course, nothing is more common than for both art and science to pay homage to the spirit of the age, or for creative taste to be ruled by prevailing taste. Where character becomes rigid and hardens itself, we can see that science strictly observes its boundaries, and art is encumbered by the heavy shackles of rules; where character becomes slack and decays, science will seek to please and art to entertain. For entire centuries both philosophers and artists have showed themselves prepared to sink truth and beauty into the depths of a depraved mankind: there philosophers and artists perish, while truth and beauty victoriously wrestle themselves upward with indestructible vitality.

The artist is certainly the child of his age, but all the worse for him if he is at the same time its pupil, even worse its minion. May a benevolent divinity tear the infant from his mother's breast and nourish him with the milk of a better age, and allow him to grow into maturity under a distant Greek sky. When he has become a man, let him return as an alien form to his own century; not to please it by his reappearance, but instead terrifying, like Agamemnon's son, to cleanse it.[1] He will take his material from the present time, but the form will come from a more refined time; indeed, beyond all time, borrowed from the absolute and immutable unity of his being. Here, from the pure ether of his daimonic nature, the spring of beauty wells, uninfected by the corruption of the generations and eras tumbling in dark eddies far below. Whim can dishonour his material just as he had ennobled it, but chaste form is beyond such flux. While in statuary the Roman of the early centuries stood erect, he had long before bent his knee to his emperor; temples were still looked upon as holy long after the gods were derided; and the misdeeds of a *Nero* and a *Commodus* were shamed by the refined style of the building which lent them cover.[2] Mankind had lost its honour, but it was rescued by art and preserved in worthy stone; truth survives in the shape of deception, and from the copy the original will be restored. Just as refined art *survived* refined nature, so the inspiration of art now goes before her, arousing and teaching her. Before truth casts its victorious light into the depths of the heart, poetic power catches its rays, and the peaks of mankind will shine out while in the valleys it is still dank night.

How does the artist shield himself from the corruptions of his age that surround him on all sides? By disdaining its judgement. He should look upwards to his dignity and the law, never downwards to fortune and need. Free both of a vain activity that would gladly leave its mark in the passing moment, and of the impatient spirit of enthusiasm that applies the measure of all things to the petty creations of the time, he may leave the sphere of the actual to the intellect, where it belongs; for he may strive instead to create the ideal by connecting the possible with the necessary. Let him express this ideal in

illusion and truth, express it in the play of his power of invention and in the gravity of his deeds, express it in all sensuous
and spiritual forms, and wordlessly project it into infinite time.

But not all in whose soul this ideal glows were granted the
creative rest and great sense of patience to imprint this ideal
upon the unnamed stone, or to pour it out in sober words,
trusting to the loyal hands of the era. Far too impetuous to
pass through this tranquil means, the divine creative impulse
often throws itself into the present and into active life, seeking to reshape the formless material of the moral world. The
misfortunes of the human race speak urgently to the sensitive
man, even more urgently its degradation; enthusiasm is roused,
and ardent yearning in vigorous souls strives impatiently for
effect. But did man not ask himself whether this disorder in the
moral world offends his reason, or perhaps instead pains his
self-love? And if he does not yet know, then he will see it in the
zeal with which it insists upon particular and prompt effects.
The pure moral impulse is directed to the absolute; for this
impulse there is no time, and the future becomes the present
once it has with necessity to develop from this present. For a
reason without limits the way is at once the destination, and
this path is completed from the moment it is commenced.

To the young friend of truth and beauty who seeks from
me knowledge of the way in which he should, despite all the
century's opposition, satisfy the noble impulse in his breast, I
say: *guide* the world upon which you act towards the good,
and the calm rhythm of time will bring about its fulfilment.
You have given the world such guidance if your teaching raises
its thoughts to the necessary and the eternal; if, by action or
example, you transform the necessary and eternal into an
object of its impulses. The edifice of delusion and capriciousness will fall, it has to fall, it has already fallen as soon as you
are certain that it is tending towards this; but this tendency
must be within man's inner self, and not merely in his external
appearance. Raise up victorious truth in the modest calm of
your soul, project it in beauty so that not only thought pays
homage to it, but sense might lovingly grasp its appearance.
And so that you might not find yourself receiving from reality

the model that you should be lending it, do not consort with its dubious company until you are assured that your heart is at one with the ideal. Live with your century, but do not be its creature; serve your contemporaries, but give them what they need, not what they praise. Without having shared their guilt, share with them with noble resignation their punishments, and bend freely under the yoke that they can hardly carry, but can hardly do without. Through the steadfast courage with which you spurn their fortune you will prove to them that it is not through cowardice that you take on their suffering. Think them how they should be when called upon to influence them; but think what they are when you are tempted to act for them. Seek their applause from their honour, but calculate their happiness according to their unworthiness; your own nobility will awake their own, and here their unworthiness will not ruin your purpose. The gravity of your principles will scare them off, but they will be able to bear them in play; their taste is purer than their heart, and here you have to grasp the timid fugitive. Their principles you will attack in vain, their acts condemn to no effect; but you can try your creative hand on their leisure. Chase from their pleasures all caprice, frivolity and coarseness; so will you imperceptibly banish them from their actions, and finally from their convictions. Wherever you find them, surround them with refined, great, inspirational forms, encircle them with symbols of excellence, until appearance conquers reality, and art nature.

TENTH LETTER

You do then agree with me, persuaded by the content of my previous letters: that man can remove himself from his destiny in two mutually opposed ways, that our era has actually taken both wrong turnings, and has fallen prey to coarseness on the one path, lethargy and perversity on the other. Having strayed along both paths, it is beauty that can lead him back. But how can fine culture deal with both contrasting failings, uniting in itself two contradictory properties? Is it capable of chaining nature in the savage, while setting it free in the barbarian? Can it at once tense and release – and if this is not actually possible, how can it reasonably be expected that beauty be capable of such a great effect as the education of mankind?

Of course, we have had to listen over and over again to the claim that a developed feeling for beauty refines morals, no further proof seeming to be here needed. Everyday experience is drawn upon for support, showing that clarity of intellect, liveliness of feeling, liberality and even the dignity of one's conduct are linked to an educated taste, and the opposite usually to an uneducated taste. The example of the most civilized of all ancient nations is confidently invoked, where the feeling for beauty reached its highest level of development; and equally confidently, example is made of the opposite, the partly savage, partly barbarian peoples who paid for their lack of sensitivity to beauty with their coarse, or in any case austere, character. All the same, thinkers have sometimes been inclined either to deny the fact or to doubt the rectitude of conclusions that can be drawn from it. They do not think so badly of the savage condition with which uncultured peoples are reproached, nor so much of the refinement for which the cultured are praised.[1] Even in Antiquity there were men who considered fine culture to be nothing less than a blessing, and were consequently very much inclined to refuse the artifices of the power of imagination entry to their republic.[2]

I am not talking here about those who spurned the Graces on the grounds that they never found favour with them. Those who have no standard of value other than the trouble of making a living and tangible profit – how should they be capable of appraising the silent labour of taste in the inner and outer man, and not ignore the material advantage of fine culture when noting its occasional disadvantage? The man without form despises all grace in appearance as bribery, all distinction of bearing as pretence, all delicacy and generosity of conduct as exaggeration and affectation. In the man on whom the Graces look with favour he cannot forgive the fact that in society such a man enlivens all acquaintances, in his worldly affairs steers all towards his own intentions, as a writer perhaps stamps his mind upon the entire century; whereas the man without form, condemned to laborious effort, can with all his knowledge compel no recognition, move no stone from its allotted place. Since he is never able to discern the genial secret of being pleasant, so there remains nothing more for him than to complain of the perversity of human nature in praising appearance before essence.

There are, however, voices raised against beauty to which one should pay attention, since they are armed with formidable arguments drawn from experience. They say: 'It cannot be denied that the charms of beauty can in good hands be employed to praiseworthy purpose, but it is not contrary to its nature that, in bad hands, it has quite the opposite effect, making its power to captivate souls serve the ends of error and injustice. Precisely because taste concerns itself with form and never with substance, ultimately it encourages the soul to neglect all reality, sacrificing truth and morality for the sake of charming appearance. All material discrimination between things is lost, and mere appearance decides their value.' They continue: 'How many men of ability are not diverted by the seductive power of beauty, or at least enticed into making light of it! How many of weak intellect are in disagreement with civil order because the imagination of poets is fond of fashioning worlds in which everything is different, in which no convention binds opinion, no artifice oppresses nature? What dangerous dialectic have the passions not acquired since poets and writers have painted them in the most glowing colours, while in the struggle with laws and duties they usually prevail? What even has society gained by beauty now making laws that were previously governed by truth, and by superficial impression commanding a regard that should instead be earned? It is true that all virtues can now be seen to blossom, some making a pleasing impact upon appearance, conferring value in society; but all the same, all kinds of excess are now flourishing, and all vice prospers that can be fitted with superficial finery.' And in fact it must prompt reflection that, in almost every historical epoch in which the arts blossom and taste reigns supreme, mankind is debased; and there is not one single example to be found in which a higher degree and a greater prevalence of aesthetic culture in a people go hand in hand with political liberty and civic virtue, where fine manners correspond to virtuous morality, the polish of conduct with the truth of the same.[3]

When *Athens* and *Sparta* retained their independence, respect for the law being the foundation of their constitutions, taste was as yet immature, artifice in its infancy, and there were many for whom beauty had no command of their souls. True, the art of poetry had already taken flight, but only with the kind of genius that borders upon savagery, a light that glimmers in obscurity, and so testifying more against than for the taste of the age. When the golden era for the arts came during the rule of Pericles and Alexander,[4] and the rule of taste became more generally diffused, the strength and liberty of Greece were already gone, rhetoric falsified truth, wisdom in the mouth of a Socrates gave offence, as did virtue in the life of a Phocion.[5] As we know, the *Romans* had first to exhaust themselves in civil wars and, emasculated through oriental luxury, submit to the yoke of a fortunate dynast before we can see the rigidity of their character overcome by Greek art.[6] Nor did culture dawn for the *Arabs*, until the energy of their warrior spirit had waned under the rule of the Abbasids.[7] In modern *Italy* the fine arts did not emerge until the glorious Lombard League was destroyed,[8] Florence subordinated to the Medicis and the spirit of independence in all valiant cities had given way to inglorious resignation. It is almost superfluous to mention the example of more recent nations whose growth in refinement matched their decline of independence. Wherever in the past we direct our gaze we discover that taste and liberty flee from each other, and that the rule of beauty is founded upon the decline of heroic virtues.

But it is just this energy of character, at whose expense aesthetic culture is usually bought, that proves itself the most effective spring of everything great and excellent in man, the lack of which nothing else, however advantageous, can replace. And so if one just bears in mind what previous experience teaches about the influence of beauty, one cannot in fact be very much encouraged to develop feelings so dangerous to the true culture of man; one would rather risk the danger of coarseness and harshness in doing without the molten power of beauty as be delivered up to its enervating effects, whatever the advantages of refinement might be. But perhaps *experience* is no sure guide in considering a question like this, and before admitting the weight of its testimony we should remove any doubt that we are talking about the same kind of beauty, against which these examples testify. However, this seems to presuppose a concept of beauty that has a source other than that of experience, since it is through this that we will be able to decide whether what in experience is called beautiful is properly so named.

This purely *rational concept* of beauty, if there is such a thing, would therefore – since it cannot be created from any actual instance, but rather corrects and guides our judgement of every actual instance – have to be sought by means of abstraction, and be capable of deduction from the possibility of sensuously rational nature; in a word: beauty would have to show itself to be a necessary condition of humanity. We must then henceforth raise our thoughts to the pure concept of humanity; and since experience only shows us discrete conditions of individual men, but never humanity itself, so we must discover from these individual and changeable phenomenal forms the absolute and the immutable, and by discarding all contingent limitations seek to master the necessary conditions of their being. Of course, this transcendental path will for a time remove us from the familiar domain of appearances and from the living presence of things, remaining for a time in the barren reaches of abstract concepts; but we seek solid ground for unshakeable knowledge, and whosoever dares not venture beyond actuality will never conquer truth.

ELEVENTH LETTER

When abstraction rises to the highest possible level it reaches two ultimate concepts, at which it must halt and recognize its limits. This distinguishes something in man that persists, and something that continually changes. The first is called *person*, and the second its *condition*.

Person and condition, the self and its determinants – we conceive these in the necessary being as one and the same, eternally twinned in the finite. For all constancy of person, its condition changes; for all change of conditions, the person remains constant. We shift from rest to activity, from affect to indifference, from agreement to contradiction; but *we* are always the same, and whatever follows directly from *us* remains. Only in the absolute subject do all determinants remain *with* the personality, because they flow *from* personality. Everything that divinity is remains so *because* it is; it is consequently everything in eternity, because it is eternal.

Because in man, as a finite being, person and condition are distinct, condition cannot be founded upon person, nor person upon condition. If the latter were true, then the person would have to change; if the first were true, condition would remain constant; and so in either case either personality or finitude would cease. It is not because we think, want and feel that we are who we are; not because of who we are that we think, want and feel. We are because we are; we feel, think and want because beyond us something other than ourselves exists.

The person has therefore to be grounded in itself, for what persists cannot flow from change; and this would bring us to the idea of the absolute as a being grounded in itself, that is, *freedom*.

Condition has to have a basis; it must *follow from something*, since it does not owe its existence to the person, therefore is not absolute; and this would in turn give us *time* as the condition of all contingent being or becoming. Time is the condition of all becoming: this is an identical statement, for it states nothing other than 'succession is the condition of something that succeeds'.

The person manifested in an eternally persistent 'I', and only in this, cannot become, cannot have a beginning in time, for time instead begins in the person, since change has to be based on something unchanging. Something has to alter itself if there is to be change; and this something cannot itself be change. By saying that the flower blooms and fades, we make the flower the constant in this transformation, lending it equally a persona in which both conditions take place. It is no objection to say that man has first to become, since man is not merely a person in general, but a person finding himself in a particular situation. But every situation, every particular being arises in time, and man as a phenomenon must make a beginning, although pure intelligence is eternal in him. In the absence of time, that is, without becoming a particular being, he would not be a particular being; his person would tend to exist, but not in fact. It is only in the sequence of his ideas that the persisting I itself becomes manifested to itself.

And so the material of activity, or the reality that the supreme Intelligence creates of itself, has first to be *received* by man; and he receives it through perception as something located externally to himself, and as something changing within himself over time. This shifting matter within him keeps company with his constant, unchanging 'I'; and the injunction laid upon him by his rational nature is to remain constantly himself despite all change, to transform all perception into experience, into the unity of knowledge, and render all of his forms of appearance in time into law for all times. He only *exists* by changing himself; and only by remaining unchanged does *he* exist. Man, imagined in his perfection, would accordingly be the steadfast unity that in the flux of change remained eternally the same.

Now, although an infinite being, a divinity, cannot *become*, one should surely call a tendency divine that had as its unending

task the most specific mark of divinity: the absolute promulga-
tion of potential (the actualization of all that is possible) and
the absolute unity of manifestation (the necessity of all that is
actual). It is indisputable that man carries within his personality the disposition to divinity; and the path to divinity – if one
can call that which never reaches its goal a path – is opened up
to him through the *senses*.

His personality, considered in itself and independently
of any sense-material, is merely the disposition for potentially infinite expression; and so long as he neither perceives
nor feels he is no more than form and empty potential. His
sensibility, considered in itself and separately from all spontaneous activity of the mind, can do no more than render
him, who in the absence of sensibility is mere form, into
matter; but in no respect can it unite him with matter. As
long as he merely feels, merely has desires, and merely acts on
his desires, he is no more than *world*, if we understand by this
term merely the formless content of time. It is indeed only
his sensibility that makes his potential into an active force;
but it is only his personality that makes his activity his own.
To be something more than mere world he must lend form to
matter; and to be more than mere form he must actualize the
disposition that he bears within himself. He realizes the form
when he brings time into existence, and counters change to
what persists, counters with the eternal unity of his self the
variety of the world; he forms matter if he annuls time once
more, affirms persistence in change and subjugates the variety
of the world to the unity of his self.

From this flow two contrasting challenges for man, the
two fundamental laws of a sensuous–rational nature. The first
insists on absolute *reality*: he should make everything that is
mere form into world, and manifest all of his dispositions.
The second insists upon absolute *formality*: he should root up
everything in himself that is mere world, harmonizing all its
changes; in other words: he should externalize all that is inte-
rior, and lend form to all that is exterior. Both tasks, conceived
in their supreme fulfilment, lead back to the concept of divinity
from which I began.

TWELFTH LETTER

For the realization of this dual task: to lend reality to the necessity *within us*, and subordinate the reality *external to us* to the rule of necessity, we are driven by two contradictory forces which, because they impel us to realize their object, are quite properly called impulses.* The first impulse, which I will call the *material impulse*,[1] derives from the physical existence of man, or from his sensuous nature, and seeks to place him under the constraints of time, making him matter; not giving him matter, for that is proper to the free activity of a person who takes up matter and distinguishes it from himself as a persisting entity. But matter is here nothing but change, or reality that fulfils time; correspondingly the material impulse demands that change shall occur, that time shall have a content. This condition of time that is merely occupied is called sensation, and it is through this alone that physical existence is made manifest.

---

* I have no reservations in using this expression both for the following of a rule and for the satisfaction of a need, however much one might otherwise tend to restrict it to the latter. In the same way, rational ideas become imperatives or obligations as soon as they are placed within the constraints of time, as soon as they are related to something definite and actual. For example, the veracity as something absolute and necessary that reason prescribes to all intelligence is actual in the Supreme Being because it is potential; for this follows from the concept of a necessary being. And this idea, when placed in the limits of humanity, of course remains necessary, if only morally, and *should* first be made actual because in a contingent being actuality is not yet determined by potentiality. If experience should provide a case to which this imperative of veracity can be related, it arouses an impulse, an endeavour, to exercise this rule, bringing about the harmony prescribed by reason with itself. This impulse necessarily arises and is not absent in those who act against it. Without it there would be no morally evil will, nor consequently morally good will.

Since everything that is in time occurs as a *succession*, the fact that something exists excludes all else. If one sounds a note on an instrument, this one note is the sole actual note among all those that this instrument could possibly make; and insofar as man senses what is present to him, the entire and infinite potentiality of his conditions is limited to this one form of existence. There is necessarily therefore the highest degree of restriction where the material impulse has exclusive effect; in this situation man is no more than a unit of quantity, a fulfilled moment of time – or rather, *he* is not, for his personality is suspended for as long as he is ruled by sensation, and swept along by time.*

The domain of this impulse reaches as far as man's finite being does; and since all form appears only as material, everything absolute only through the medium of constraint, it is certainly this material impulse to which the entire phenomenon of mankind is ultimately bound. But although it is this impulse alone that rouses and develops the dispositions of mankind, it is him alone that makes their fulfilment impossible. It irrevocably shackles the flight of mind to the sensuous world, calling abstraction back from the most unconstrained and infinite excursion into the constraints of the present. Thought may for a moment escape, and a determined will triumphantly resist its demands; but soon a suppressed nature will resume its rights, insisting on the reality of existence, on the content of our knowledge and the purpose of our action.

The second of these impulses, which can be called the *formal impulse*,[2] is based upon the absolute existence of man, or upon his rational nature; it seeks to set him at liberty, bring

---

* There is a very appropriate expression for this loss of self when under the sway of sensation: *to be beside oneself*, to be outside one's self. Although this turn of speech is used only where sensation becomes affect, and this condition becomes more noticeable by longer duration, in fact everyone is beside himself for as long as he does nothing but feel. The return from this condition to one of self-possession is called equally appropriately: *to be oneself* again, to return into oneself, to restore his person. One does not say of people who have fainted that they are 'beside themselves', but rather someone is, 'out', he has lost consciousness, is not himself. Hence someone who recovers from fainting 'comes to', a state which is quite compatible with being 'beside oneself'.

harmony to the variety of his appearance and affirm his person amidst all change of condition. Since the last of these, as an absolute and indivisible unity, can never be in contradiction with itself, *since we are for all eternity we ourselves*, the impulse that strives to maintain personality can never demand anything other than what it must for all eternity claim; it decides for ever as it decides for the present, and commands for the present what it will always command. With this it also enfolds the entire succession of time, which is to say: it annuls time, and annuls change; it wishes to make the actual necessary and eternal, and the eternal and necessary actual; in other words, it insists upon truth and right.

While the material impulse only provides *cases*, the formal impulse provides *laws*; laws for every judgement if it concerns knowledge, and laws for every will if it concerns actions. Suppose that we recognize an object, that we attribute objective validity to a condition of our subject; or that we act upon knowledge, making an objective principle the motivation of our condition – in either case we tear this condition from the jurisdiction of time, and allow it reality for all men and all time, allow it generality and necessity. Feeling can only say: that is true *for this subject* and *for this moment*; and another moment will come, and another subject, revoking the expression of present feeling. But if the thought is once stated: *that is*, then it decides for ever and eternity, and the validity of its utterance is guaranteed by personality itself, which defies all change. Inclination can only say: that suits *your individuality* and *your present need*, but your individuality and your present need will be swept away with change, and what you today fiercely desire will in time become the object of your disgust. If, however, moral feeling says: *that shall be*, then it decides for ever and eternity – if you admit truth because it is truth, and practise justice because it is just, then you have made one single case the rule for all cases, and treated one moment in your life as eternity.

Where therefore the formal impulse rules, and the pure object acts within us, that is the supreme extension of being, all barriers disappear, man has elevated a unit of quantity, to which meagre sense had limited him, into a *unity of ideas* that comprehends the entire realm of phenomena. With this operation we are no longer in time, but instead time is within us, with its never-ending succession. We are no longer individuals, but a species; the judgement of all minds is expressed by our own, the choice of all hearts is represented through our deed.

THIRTEENTH LETTER

At first glance nothing seems to be more contradictory than the tendencies of these two impulses, the one striving for change, and the other for immutability. Nonetheless, it is these two impulses that exhaust the concept of humanity, and a third *basic impulse* that could reconcile the two is quite simply unthinkable. How can we then restore the unity of human nature, which seems to have been shattered by this original and radical contradiction?

It is true that their *tendencies* contradict each other, but we should note, not in the *same objects*, and what never meets cannot collide. The material impulse does demand change, but it does not demand that change extend to the person and its domain: a change of basic principles. The formal impulse strives for unity and persistence – but in seeking to fix the person it does not seek to fix the conditions, does not require the identity of sensation. Nature does not therefore set them against each other, and if that appears to be so, this has happened through a free encroachment of nature, mistaking their nature and confusing their spheres.* The task of *culture*

---

* Once one asserts that an original and hence necessary antagonism exists between the two impulses, there is of course no way in which the unity of man can be maintained other than by unconditionally *subordinating* the sensuous impulse to the rational. While mere uniformity can arise from this, harmony cannot, man remaining eternally divided. Subordination there has to be, but reciprocally: for if limitations can never be the foundation for the absolute, that freedom can never depend upon time, it is just as certain that the absolute can never of itself be the foundation for limitation, that the condition in time cannot be dependent upon freedom. Both principles are at once subordinated to each other, and co-ordinated; they relate reciprocally – without form, no matter; without matter, no form. (This concept of reciprocity and its entire

is to watch over them, securing the limits of each impulse; it
has an equal duty of justice to both, not simply to the formal
impulse in regard to the material impulse, but also the latter in
regard to the former. It therefore has a dual task: *firstly*, preserving sensibility from the encroachments of liberty; *secondly*,
securing personality against the power of sensations. The first
is achieved by developing the capacity for feeling, the second
by developing the capacity for reason.

Since the world is extended in time, is therefore change, the
perfection of that faculty that connects men to the world must
have the greatest capacity to change and extend. Since the person is the constant when change occurs, then the perfection of
that faculty that is to counter change must have the greatest
possible autonomy and intensity. The more aspects there are to
man's receptivity, the more flexible it is and the greater the
number of aspects presented to phenomena, so the greater
the amount of the world that man can *grasp*, the more faculties
he develops within himself. The more power and depth that
personality gains, the more freedom that reason gains, so the
more world does man *comprehend*, so the more form he creates outside of himself. His culture would therefore consist of:
firstly, bringing about the most varied contact with the world
for the receptive faculty, while intensifying as far as possible
passivity in feeling; *secondly*, securing for the determining

---

importance is subjected to excellent analysis in Fichte's *Grundlage der ges-
ammten Wissenschaftslehre* (Leipzig 1794).) We do not, of course, know how
it stands with the person in the realm of ideas; however, we certainly do know
that in the absence of matter the person cannot manifest itself in the realm of
time. And so in the realm of time matter will have something to determine;
not as merely *subordinate* to form, but in addition *alongside* it, and independent of it. However necessary it may be that feeling should not influence the
domain of reason, it is equally necessary that reason not influence the domain
of feeling. Simply by lending each a domain for themselves each is excluded
from the other; setting a limit to each that can be infringed only *to the disadvantage of both*.

In a transcendental philosophy concerned above all with freeing form from
content, and the necessary from everything contingent, one can easily come to
think of matter simply as an obstacle; and sensibility, just because it represents
an obstruction in *this* particular issue, to be necessarily in contradiction with
reason. This kind of idea is certainly not part of the *spirit* of the Kantian
system, but it could well be found in its *letter*.

faculty the greatest independence from the receptive faculty, developing reason to the greatest possible degree of activity. Where both qualities are united, man will combine the most abundant existence with the greatest autonomy and liberty and, rather than losing himself in the world, instead draw into himself the sheer infinity of its phenomena and subordinate it to the unity of his reason.

Now man can *overturn* this relation, and so fail to realize his destiny in two ways. He can transfer the intensity required by his active powers to his passive powers, allowing the material impulse to encroach upon the formal impulse, and make his receptive capacity determinant. Or he can transfer the extension proper to the passive powers to his active powers, the formal impulse then encroaching upon the sensuous, and substitute the determinant capacity for the receptive. In the first case he never becomes *he himself*; in the second he never becomes *something other*; and so in each case he is *neither the one nor the other*, and consequently a nonentity.*

* The harmful influence on our thought and action of an overweening sensuousness is obvious to all; but it is not so easy to see whether an overweening rationality equally frequently and importantly has a disadvantageous influence upon our knowledge and conduct. Among the great number of relevant cases here, permit me therefore to note just two which illuminate the damage inflicted when thought and volition encroach upon perception and sensibility.

One of the principal reasons that our natural sciences develop at such a slow pace is quite plainly the general and barely controllable propensity for teleological judgement, which, as soon as it is used constitutively, subordinates the determining capacity to the receptive. However emphatically and frequently nature might impress itself upon our organs, all nature's variety is lost upon us because we seek in it only what we have already placed there, because we do not allow it to *move into us*, but instead *thrust ourselves upon it*, employing an impatient and interfering reason. If centuries later someone comes along whose senses are calm, innocent and open, and so stumbles on a quantity of phenomena that our prejudice has caused us to ignore, then we are amazed that so many eyes could in broad daylight have missed so much. This premature striving for harmony before one has registered the individual tones from which it is made, the monstrous usurpation by the power of thought of a domain that it in no respect commands, is the reason that so many thinkers fail to further the best of science, and it is hard to say which has harmed the extension of knowledge the more: a faculty of sense lacking all form, or a faculty of reason that cannot wait for content.

If the material impulse is in the ascendant, sense ruling, and the world suppresses the person, then the world ceases to be an object to the degree that it becomes a force. As soon as man is merely the substance of time *he* ceases to exist, and as a consequence he *has* no substance. With the annulment of his personality his condition is also annulled, because both are mutually related concepts – for change needs something that remains fixed, and a limited reality demands an infinite one. If the formal impulse becomes receptive, if the power of thought forestalls that of sensation, and if the person displaces the world, so it ceases by the same measure to be an autonomous power and a subject so far as it forces itself into the place of

It is just as difficult to determine whether our practical philanthropy is more disturbed by the strength of our desires than chilled through the rigidity of our principles; disturbed more by the egoism of our senses than chilled by that of our reason. Feeling and character are together needed to make us compassionate, helpful, active men and women, just as, to gain experience, openness of the senses and an energy of intellect must come together. How can we be true to such praiseworthy maxims as being just, kindly and humane to others if we lack the capacity to accept alien nature into ourselves truly and faithfully, to adapt to alien situations, to make the feelings of others our own? But this capacity – both in the education we are given and in that which we give ourselves – is suppressed to the same degree that we seek to break the power of desires, and reinforce character by principles. Since feeling is so easily stirred, it is with difficulty that one remains true to one's principles; and so one reaches for an easier path, securing character by blunting feelings; for it is certainly infinitely easier to be at ease when faced with a disarmed adversary than in seeking to overwhelm one who is armed and spirited. In this operation we find the greater part of what is called *forming a man*; and in the best sense of the word, involving work on the inner man, and not simply the outer. A man shaped in this manner will certainly be immune from being of crude nature, and appearing as such; he will at the same time be armoured through principles against all natural impulses, and mankind will neither approximate to him *from without* nor *from within*.

The ideal of perfection is subjected to the most pernicious misuse if it is employed with all rigour in the judgement of other men, and in cases where one has to act on their behalf. The first leads to sentimental enthusiasm, the latter to hardness and coldness. One takes one's social obligations very lightly if the *actual* man who claims our help is displaced in our thought by an *ideal man* who could probably help himself. The truly impressive character is one that combines rigour for oneself with tender-heartedness for others. However, usually the man who is tender with others is also soft on himself, and he who is strict with himself is also strict with others; while to be soft on oneself and strict with others is the most despicable character.

the object, since, to be made manifest, what persists demands change, and absolute reality requires limits. Once man becomes form, then he *has* no form; and the annulment of his condition is consequently that of his person too. In a word: only to the extent that he is autonomous is reality external to him, is he receptive; only to the extent that he is receptive is reality in him, is he a thinking force.

Both material impulse and formal impulse have limits and, insofar as they can be thought of as energy, they are in need of relaxation: for the material impulse, so that it does not penetrate the domain of law; for the formal impulse, so that it does not penetrate the domain of sensation. Any relaxation of the material impulse must not, however, result from physical incapacity and a dulling of the senses, for everywhere this meets with contempt; it has to be an action made in liberty, an activity of the person whose moral intensity moderates the sensuous and, by mastering impressions, robs them of depth while lending them space. Character must set bounds to temperament, for sense can concede *only to mind*. Nor should that relaxation of the formal impulse be the effect of intellectual incapacity and slackness in powers of thought or will, which would degrade mankind. A wealth of sensations must be its laudable source; sensibility itself must lay victorious claim to its domain, and resist the violence that the mind would inflict through encroaching upon it. In a word: personality must keep the material impulse within its proper bounds, as the formal impulse must be by receptivity, or nature.

FOURTEENTH LETTER

We have been led to the concept of a reciprocity between the two impulses in which the effects of the one both found and limit the effects of the other, and in which each achieves its greatest manifestation through the activity of the other.

This reciprocity between both impulses is, of course, nothing but a task assigned to reason, but a task which man is only able to solve completely in the perfection of his existence. It is in the most proper sense of the word *the idea of his humanity*, consequently something infinite to which he can in time approach ever more closely, without, however, ever reaching it. 'He should not strive for form at the cost of his reality, nor for reality at the cost of form; rather, he should seek absolute being through determinate being, and determinate being through infinite being. He should confront the world because he is a person, and shall be a person because a world confronts him. He should feel because he is conscious of himself, and shall be conscious of himself because he feels.' He cannot truly fulfil this idea – be a man in the fullest sense of the word – as long as he seeks to satisfy just one of these impulses, or one after the other; for while he only feels then his person or absolute existence remains hidden from him, and while he only thinks then his existence in time, or condition, is likewise hidden from him. If, however, there were cases in which he were to have this dual experience *simultaneously*, where he was both conscious of his liberty and sensed his existence, where he felt himself to be matter while knowing himself as mind, then he would have in these cases, and only in these cases, complete perception of his humanity; and the object that this perception gave him would become for him a symbol of his *accomplished destiny*, consequently serving as a representation of the infinite (since this can only be attained in the totality of time).

Assuming that cases of this kind can arise in experience, they would arouse a new impulse in man; and since the two other impulses are conjoined within this new impulse, it would be opposed to each of them separately, and so quite properly taken for a new impulse. The material impulse seeks change, desires that time has a content; the formal impulse seeks to annul time, desires that nothing changes. This new impulse, the sensuous and the formal working within it (until such time as I have justified such a name, allow me to call it the *playful impulse*) – this playful impulse aims at the annulment of time *within time*, uniting becoming with absolute being, and change with identity.[1]

The material impulse seeks to *be* defined, it seeks to receive its object; the formal impulse seeks to define *itself*, it seeks to create its object; and so the playful impulse will strive to receive as if it had created itself, and create in such a way as to be received by the senses as such. It could be said that the material impulse aims at multiplying unity in time, because sensation is a succession of realities; the formal impulse aims at uniting diversity in the idea, since thought is the concurrence of the different; the playful impulse will bring about the multiplication in time of the unity of the idea; make law into feeling; or what is much the same, unite diversity in time in the idea, making feeling law.

The material impulse excludes from its subject all autonomy and liberty, while the formal impulse excludes all dependency, all passivity. Exclusion of freedom is, however, a physical necessity, while the exclusion of passivity is a moral one. Both impulses therefore constrain the soul, the first by the laws of nature, the second by laws of reason. Hence the playful impulse, in which both of these impulses work in tandem, constrains the soul both morally and physically; since it annuls all contingency, it therefore annuls all constraint and sets man physically and morally free. If we embrace someone passionately who deserves our contempt we are pained by the *compulsion of nature*. If we feel enmity towards someone who demands our regard, then we are pained by the *compulsion of reason*. But as soon as he has both engaged our affection and gained our regard, the compulsion of both sensation and conscience disappears, and we begin to love him, that is, play with both our affection and our regard.

Since, then, the material impulse constrains us physically, and the formal impulse morally, the first leaves our formal disposition to contingency, as the latter likewise leaves our material disposition; it is a matter of chance whether our happiness conforms with our perfection, or the latter with the former. The playful impulse, in which both work together, will render contingent both our formal and material disposition, and at the same time our perfection and our happiness; in making *both* contingent, and because along with necessity contingency also disappears, it will annul contingency in both, bringing form to matter and reality to form. To the same degree that it deprives sensations and affects of their dynamic influence it will bring them into conformity with ideas of reason; and to the same degree as it deprives the laws of reason of their moral compulsion it will reconcile them with the interest of the senses. Under its rule the pleasant will become an object, and the good a power. It will exchange in its *object* matter with form, and form with matter; in its *subject* it will transform necessity into liberty, and liberty into necessity, and in this way place them within man in the deepest community.

FIFTEENTH LETTER

I am nearing the goal to which I am leading you on a path that offers little by way of cheer. If you would be so good as to follow me a few steps further, a wider perspective will open up, and a pleasing prospect that will perhaps make all your effort worthwhile.

Expressed as a general concept, the object of the material impulse is called *life*, in its widest meaning: a concept signifying all material being, everything directly present to the senses. The object of the formal impulse, expressed again as a general concept, is called *form*, both in the figurative and the literal sense of the word: a concept that includes all the formal properties of things, and all of their relations to the powers of thought. The object of the playful impulse, presented in general outline, can consequently be called *living form*: a concept serving to characterize all aesthetic properties of phenomena, what is in a word most generally called *beauty*.

In this explanation, if such it is, beauty is neither extended to the entire domain of the living, nor restricted only to this domain. A block of marble, although it remains lifeless, can all the same assume living form in the hands of an architect or sculptor; while a man, although he lives and has form, is far from being living form by virtue of this. For that, his form has to be life, and his life form. So long as we merely think of his form it is lifeless, a mere abstraction; so long as we merely feel his life, it lacks form, is a mere impression. Only by his form living in our senses, and his life forming itself in our intellect, is he a living form, and that will always be the case whenever we judge him to be beautiful.

The fact that we know how to name the parts that, in their union, create beauty, in no respect explains its genesis; for this would require that *this union itself* was understood, and this remains unknowable to us, as with all reciprocity between the finite and the infinite. Reason makes the following demand on transcendental grounds: let there be community between formal impulse and material impulse – in other words, a playful impulse, because only the unity of reality and form, contingency with necessity, passivity with freedom completes the concept of mankind. It has to make this demand because it is reason – because by its nature it insists upon perfection and the removal of all barriers, and all exclusive activity of one or the other impulse leaves human nature imperfect, and creates a limit within it. Accordingly, as soon as reason has pronounced: let mankind exist, by so doing it has created the law: let beauty exist. Experience can tell us *whether* a beauty is such, and we will know it as soon as it has taught us whether a mankind exists. But *how* a beauty can exist, and how a mankind is possible, this neither reason nor experience can teach us.

We know that man is neither exclusively matter, nor exclusively mind. Hence beauty, as the consummation of his humanity, cannot be exclusively an object of the material impulse, be mere life, as has been claimed by quick-witted observers who adhered too closely to the testimony of experience, and to which the taste of the times would gladly reduce it; nor can it be exclusively an object of the formal impulse, mere form, as maintained by speculative philosophers too far removed from experience, and by philosophizing artists whose explanation of beauty was too heavily dependent upon the needs of art;[*1] it is the common object of both impulses: of the play-

* *Burke* makes beauty mere life in his *Philosophical Enquiry into the Origin of Our Ideas of the Sublime and Beautiful.* As far as I am aware, every adherent of the *dogmatic* system who has expressed himself on this matter makes it pure form; among the artists *Raphael Mengs*, in his *Thoughts on Taste in Painting*; not to mention others. As in everything else, *Critical* Philosophy has here also opened up a path through which empiricism can be led back to principles, and speculation to experience.

ful impulse. The term finds complete justification in linguistic usage, which tends to use the word 'play' for everything that is neither subjectively nor objectively contingent, and yet imposes no constraint, either inwardly or outwardly. Since the soul, when contemplating the beautiful, finds itself in a happy medium between law and need, it is freed of the constraint of the one as well as the other since it is divided between the two. The material impulse, like the formal impulse, is entirely *serious* in its demands, since the first relates, in knowledge, to reality, and the second to the necessity of things; because, in acting, the first is directed to the maintenance of life, and the second to the preservation of dignity, both therefore being directed to truth and perfection. But life becomes more indifferent, the more that dignity takes part, and duty is no longer an obligation once it is subject to inclination; in like manner the soul accepts the reality of things, material truth, with greater freedom and serenity as soon as it meets formal truth, the law of necessity, and no longer feels itself constrained by abstraction as soon as direct intuition can accompany it. In a word: by coming into association with ideas everything actual loses its earnestness, for it becomes *petty*; and insofar as it encounters sensation the necessary loses its earnestness, because it becomes *easy*.

You have probably long wanted to object that by making beauty the mere object of play I have degraded it, equating it with frivolous things that have always been such objects. Does it not contradict the concept of reason and the dignity of beauty, which is after all considered to be an instrument of culture, to reduce it to *mere play*, and does it not contradict our experience of play, which can exist independently of any taste, that it be limited just to beauty?

But then what is *mere* play, once we know that under all conditions of man it is exactly play, and *only* play, that makes him complete, and begins to develop his dual nature? What you, following your own ideas of the matter, call *limitation*, I, according to my own ideas and which I have justified through proof, call *extension*. I would instead maintain the opposite: man is *only* in earnest when it comes to the pleasant, the good, the perfect; but when it comes to beauty he plays.* Of course, we do not here have in mind games that take place in real life, and which are usually directed only towards very material objects; but we should also seek vainly in real life for the kind of beauty we are discussing here. Actually existing beauty is what the actually existing playful impulse deserves; but the ideal of beauty that reason sets up also relinquishes an ideal of the playful impulse which man should have clearly in mind in all his playing. Depending on whether the playful impulse is closer to the material impulse or the formal, beauty will also be closer to mere life or to mere form; and one will never err in seeking a man's ideal of beauty thus, in the way in which he satisfies his impulse to play. If the Greek people diverted themselves during their Olympian games with bloodless competitions of strength, speed and agility, and the more noble rivalries of talent, and if the Roman people relished the death throes of a beaten gladiator or of his Libyan opponent, it becomes clear to us why we have to seek the ideal forms of a Venus, a Juno, an Apollo not in Rome, but in Greece.† But now reason tells us: the beautiful should not be mere life and not mere form, but instead living form, that is beauty; for of course it dictates to man the dual law of absolute formality and of absolute reality. And so reason also says: the playful impulse should be neither mere material impulse, nor mere formal impulse, but both at the same time – which is the playful impulse. In other words: man should *only play* with beauty, and he should play *only with beauty*.

And so at long last, to state it clearly and completely: man plays only when he is a man in the full sense of the word,

---

* There are card games (*Chartenspiel*) and tragedies (*Trauerspiel*); but quite obviously the game of cards is much too *serious* for this name.

† If (keeping with the modern world) we compare horse-racing in London, bull-fights in Madrid, the *spectacles* in the Paris of times past, the gondola races in Venice, animal-baiting in Vienna, and the happy atmosphere of Rome's Corso, then it is not hard to determine the differing shades of taste existing between these different peoples. However, there is far less uniformity among the common pursuits of the people in these different countries than there is among the amusements of the more refined classes in the very same countries, which is easy to explain.

and *he is only a complete man when he plays*. This statement, which might now perhaps seem paradoxical, gains significance and depth when we come to relate it to the dual earnestness of duty and fate; I promise you that it will support the entire edifice of aesthetic art and of the difficult art of living. But this statement is only unexpected in the sciences; it has long been accepted in the arts, and in the feelings of the Greeks, the most refined masters of all art; except that they consigned to Olympus what should have happened on earth. Guided by its truth, they banished from the brow of the blessed gods all the gravity and labour that furrow the cheeks of mortals, together with the frivolous pleasures that smooth empty faces, freed those who were eternally content from the fetters of any purpose, any obligation, any cares, making *idleness* and *indifference* the envied lot of the gods: simply a more humane name for the freest, most sublime being. Both the material constraint of the laws of nature and the spiritual constraint of moral laws were resolved into the higher concept of necessity including both worlds, and it was from the unity of both these necessities that true liberty first arose. Inspired by this spirit, the Greeks eliminated from their ideal countenance all trace of both *inclination* and *volition*; or rather, they rendered both unrecognizable, since they knew how to connect them in the most intimate bond. It is neither grace, nor is it dignity, that speaks to us in the wonderful face of a *Juno Ludovisi*;[2] it is neither the one nor the other, because it is at once both. This goddess, by demanding our veneration, kindles our love for the god-like woman; but while we abandon ourselves to her heavenly blessedness, so we recoil from her heavenly self-sufficiency. The entire form reposes within itself, an entirely complete and self-contained creation, as if she were beyond space, unyielding, unresisting; there is no force here that fights other powers, no weak spot where temporality might break in. Irresistibly drawn in by the first, while kept at a distance by the second, we find ourselves at once in a state of complete rest and complete movement, and that wonderful arousal develops for which intellect has no concept, and language no name.

SIXTEENTH LETTER

We have seen how the beautiful emerges from the reciprocity of two contrary impulses, and from the connection of two contrary principles; and whose supreme ideal is thus to be found in the most perfected bond and *equilibrium* of reality and form. This equilibrium can, however, remain only an idea that reality can never quite achieve. In reality, one element will always outweigh the other; and the most that we can expect from experience is a *fluctuation* between both principles, in which now reality, now form is preponderant. Beauty as an idea is therefore eternally an indivisible unity, because there can be only one single equilibrium; by contrast, beauty in experience will always be dual, because fluctuation can disturb the equilibrium, now to one side, then the other.

In one of my earlier letters I remarked, and it can be rigorously deduced from what I have written so far, that we might expect from the beautiful an effect both of release and of tensioning: a *releasing* effect, to keep both sensuous and formal impulses within bounds; and a *tensioning* effect, to maintain the powers of each. Ideally, however, these two effects of beauty should be one and the same. Beauty should release, so that both natures might be equally tensioned; and it should be tensioned, so that both might be equally released. By working together with the sensuous and the formal impulses they each draw their own boundaries; and in that each holds the other to its limits, beauty has given to both their proper liberty. This follows from the concept of reciprocity, by virtue of which both parts simultaneously and necessarily condition each other and are conditioned by each other, the purest

product of which is beauty. However, experience offers us no
such example of perfect reciprocity; instead it will always turn
out that a preponderance will to a greater or lesser extent
give rise to a deficiency, and a deficiency to a preponderance.
Hence, what then is for the ideal of beauty a distinction *made*
in imagination *is* for the beauty found in experience an exis-
tential difference. The ideal of beauty, although indivisible and
simple, evinces in its different relationships a property both
liquifying and energetic; while in experience *there is* liquifying
and energetic beauty.[1] That is the way it is, and that is the way
it will always be in all cases where the absolute is subject to the
limits of time, and ideas of reason are to be realized in mankind. The reflective man thinks in this way about virtue, truth
and happiness; but the active man will simply practise *virtue*,
simply grasp *truth*, and simply enjoy *happy days*. To link these
experiences to the former abstractions – putting morality in the
place of morals, knowledge in the place of what is known, happiness in the place of good fortune – is the business of physical
and moral culture; making beauty out of beautiful things is the
task of aesthetic culture.

Energetic beauty can as little preserve men from a certain
residue of savagery and hardness as it can protect liquifying
beauty from a certain degree of softening and enervation. For
since the effect of the first is to brace the soul physically and
morally, increasing its powers of response, so it happens all too
easily that the resistance of temperament and character reduces
receptivity to impressions, so that even the most delicate
humanity undergoes a repression meant only for raw nature;
and raw nature shares a gain in strength meant only for the free
person; so it is for this reason that one finds in times of strength
and abundance the true greatness of imagination paired with
the gigantic and the extravagant, and the sublimity of conviction paired with the most appalling outbreaks of passion; so it
is that in times of rule and form nature is just as often oppressed
as mastered, just as often offended as transcended. And because
the effect of liquifying beauty is to soften the soul both morally
and physically, it as easily comes about that the energy of feeling is smothered along with the force of the appetites, and that

character also experiences a loss of power that is meant only to affect passion; and so in what are thought to be more refined eras it is not rare for gentleness to become softness, breadth to become shallowness, correctness to become empty formality, liberality to become arbitrariness, making light of things frivolity, calm to become apathy, and to see the most despicable caricatures in the closest proximity to the most wonderful humanity. Liquifying beauty is therefore a need for man constrained either by form or by matter; for before he begins to be receptive to harmony and grace he has long been moved by greatness and power. For the man ruled by the indulgence of taste energetic beauty is a need, for when in a condition of refinement he is only too ready to squander a strength that he retained from the condition of savagery.

And so I think that the contradiction that one commonly encounters in the opinion of men about the influence of the beautiful, and in their appreciation of aesthetic culture, has been explained and answered. The contradiction is explained as soon as one recalls that there are in experience two kinds of beauty, and that both parts claim a whole that each is capable of demonstrating itself only in part. This contradiction is removed once we distinguish the dual need of mankind to which this dual beauty corresponds. Both parts will probably prove to be right, if only they can first agree between themselves which kind of beauty and which form of mankind they have in mind.

I will therefore, in the continuation of my investigations, assume as my own the path that nature takes with man in aesthetic matters, deriving the general concept of beauty from its two kinds. I will examine the effect of liquifying beauty on the tensioned man, and the effect of energetic beauty on the relaxed man, so that I might finally resolve both contrary kinds of beauty into the unity of the ideal-beautiful, as the two contrary forms of mankind resolve into the unity of the ideal man.

LIQUIFYING BEAUTY
SEVENTEENTH LETTER

So long as it was merely a matter of deducing the general idea of beauty from the concept of human nature, we were unable to think of any limitation of the latter that was not founded directly on its essence, and which is inseparable from the concept of finitude. Disregarding the contingent limitations to which human nature was subject in its actual manifestations, we deduced its concept directly from reason, the source of all necessity; and with this, the ideal of mankind was formed along with the ideal of beauty.

But now we descend from the region of ideas to the arena of actuality, encountering man *in a determinate* condition, together with limitations that do not come from his simple concept, but flow from his external circumstances and the contingent use of his freedom. Whatever may be the varied ways in which the idea of mankind is contained within him, the basic content of this teaches us that, altogether, there can be only *two* contrary deviations from it. If his perfection consists in harmonizing the energy of his sensuous and intellectual powers, then any shortfall in this perfection must be due either to a lack of harmony or to a lack of energy. Hence even before we have questioned the witnesses of experience about this, we have already established by pure reason that actual (limited) man will find himself in a state either of tension or of relaxation, depending upon how the independent activity of individual forces disturbs the harmony of his being, or the unity of his nature arises from the uniform slackening of his sensuous and intellectual powers. As

will now be demonstrated, both contrary limits will be elevated
by beauty, restoring harmony to the tense man and vitality to
the relaxed man; and in this way, in accordance with its nature,
leading a limited condition back to an absolute one, rendering
man perfectly complete in himself.*[1]

Thus beauty conceived in reality in no way belies the concept we have already formed of it in speculation; only that,
here in reality, it has much less freedom than it had in speculation, where we might apply it to the pure concept of mankind.
The man presented to beauty by experience is material already
spoiled and recalcitrant, who robs it of so much of its *ideal*
perfection when mixing it with his *individual* character. It is
consequently everywhere in reality only a special and limited
species, never a pure genus; in tensed souls it dispenses with
its freedom and diversity, while in relaxed souls it loses its
vitality, but now that we have become familiar with beauty's
genuine character we will not be confused by this contradictory
appearance. Far from defining its concept in terms of individual experience, as do the great majority, hence making *beauty*
responsible for the faults that man displays under its influence,
we know that it is man who transfers to beauty the imperfection
of his individuality, so creating an insuperable obstacle in his
subjective limitation of its perfection, reducing its absolute ideal
to two limited forms of its appearance.

Fluid beauty, it has been said, is for tense souls; energizing
beauty for relaxed souls. However, I call the man tense both
when he is driven by sensations (under the unilateral power of
the material impulse) and also when he is driven by concepts
(under the unilateral power of the formal impulse). All *exclusive* domination of either one of his basic impulses is for him
a condition of compulsion and force; liberty consists only in
the concurrence of his two natures, in the harmony of both

* The excellent author of *Principles of Aesthetics etc.* (Erfurt, 1791) distinguishes in beauty the two basic principles of *grace* and *vitality*, making beauty
the most perfect union of both: coinciding exactly with the explanation given
here. His definition thus already states the basis for the division of beauty
into a fluid beauty, comprising grace, and an energetic form, in which vitality
predominates.

necessities. The man unilaterally ruled by his feelings, or led by his senses, is therefore released and liberated by form; the man unilaterally dominated by rules, or led by intellect, is released and liberated by matter. Liquifying beauty, to meet this dual task, will show itself in two distinct guises. *Firstly*, its tranquil form will calm the wildness of life, creating a bridge from sensations to thoughts. *Secondly*, as a living image it will arm a shrunken form with sensuous power, guiding the concept back to intuition, and rule to feeling. The first service is performed for the man of nature, the second for the man of artifice. But since in both cases it does not have complete control of its human material, but rather depends upon that offered either by formless nature or by unnatural artifice, so in each case it will bear the marks of its origins, losing itself more in material life here, in empty form there.

To be able to form a concept of how beauty can become a medium through which this dual tension can be removed we must investigate its origin in the human soul. Please allow me to remain a little longer in the domain of speculation before leaving it for good, so that we might then set out into the field of experience with a firm tread.

EIGHTEENTH LETTER

Through liquifying beauty sensuous man is introduced to form and thought; through liquifying beauty the intellectual man is led back to matter, and the world of sense is restored to him.

From this it seems to follow that there must be a *happy medium* between matter and form, between passivity and action, and for us beauty is found at this point. For the majority of men this is the image that they have of beauty, once they have begun to think about its effects; all experience points to this. On the other hand, there is nothing more absurd and contradictory than a concept of this kind, since there is an *infinite* distance between matter and form, between passive and active, between sensation and thought; and nothing can bridge this distance. How do we deal with this contradiction? Beauty connects the two contrary conditions of sensation and thought, and yet there is no intermediary between them. The first is secured by experience; the second directly through reason.

This is the very point on which the whole question of beauty must ultimately turn; and if we succeed in finding a satisfactory resolution to this problem, then we will have found the thread that will guide us through the entire labyrinth of aesthetics.

Everything here depends upon two quite different operations which, in this study, must necessarily support each other. It is said that beauty connects two circumstances together *that are opposed to each other*, and which can never be united. We have to start out from this opposition; we must register and recognize it in all its purity and rigour, so that both circumstances are quite precisely differentiated; otherwise we combine things, but do not unite them. Secondly, it is said:

beauty *combines* these two opposed circumstances, so doing away with the opposition. However, since both conditions remain eternally in opposition, they can only be combined by annulling them. Our second task is therefore to render this connection complete, to make it so pure and seamless that both circumstances entirely vanish into a third, and that no trace of the former division remains in the whole; otherwise all we do is to individualize, and not unite. All the arguments that have ever prevailed in the world of philosophy concerning the concept of beauty, and to some extent still so prevail today, have no other source than this: either inquiry did not begin with a sufficiently rigorous distinction or it was not pursued to the point where a completely pure union was achieved. Those philosophers who, in thinking about this subject, allow themselves to be led blindly by their *feeling*, are incapable of making a *concept* out of beauty, because in the totality of sense impressions they cannot distinguish individual elements. Other philosophers, entrusting themselves exclusively to intellect, are incapable of forming a concept of *beauty*, because in regarding its totality they see nothing but parts; mind and matter, even in their most complete unity, remain for them eternally distinct. The first set of philosophers fear that if they should make a distinction between that which is, in feeling, actually connected, they will abolish beauty *dynamically*, as an effective force; the second set of philosophers fear that they would abolish beauty *logically*, as a concept, if they were to merge together that which the intellect considers separate. The former want to think of beauty in terms of its effects; the latter want beauty to behave in the way that they think of it. And so both miss the truth: the former, because they seek to mimic infinite nature with their limited capacity for thought; the latter, because they want to limit infinite nature to the laws of their thought. The first believe they could rob beauty of its liberty by an excessively rigorous dissection; the second, that an excessively ambitious synthesis could destroy the precision of their concept. However, the former never consider that liberty, which they quite rightly view as the essence of liberty, is not lawlessness but a harmony of laws, not arbitrariness but a supreme inner necessity; the latter never consider that the exactitude which they with equal justice demand of beauty consists not in the *exclusion of particular realities*, but in the *absolute inclusion of all*; that it is therefore not limitation but infinity. We will avoid the rocks on which both have foundered if we start from the two elements into which beauty divides in the intellect, but then ascend to the pure aesthetic unity through which it affects sensation, and in which both of these circumstances entirely disappear.*

---

* An attentive reader would have remarked of the comparison offered here that *sensuous* aesthetes, for whom the testimony of sensation is of higher value than reasoning, are *in practice* far less removed from the truth than their opponents, although they are no match for them when it comes to *perspicacity*; and this is a relationship between nature and science that we can find everywhere. Everywhere nature (the senses) unites, while intellect discriminates; but reason reunites them. Hence man, before he begins to philosophize, is closer to truth than the philosopher who has yet to bring his investigation to a conclusion by working through all categories. It is therefore possible, without further consideration, to declare that a philosophical argument is in error once it has, *with regard to results*, contravened common sensation; but by the same token, it can be considered suspect if in form and method it conforms to this common sensation. This latter point may console the writer unable to present a philosophical deduction in the casual manner of fireside conversation, as many readers expect. The former point might silence anybody who seeks to found new systems at the expense of common sense.

NINETEENTH LETTER

Man as such can be defined in respect of two states, the passive and the active; and so we can likewise distinguish two conditions, of passive and active determination. By explaining this statement we can find the shortest path to our objective.

The condition of the human mind *before* any determination given to it through sensory impression is one of a limitless capacity to be shaped and defined. The sheer endlessness of space and time is at the free disposal of its powers of imagination; and since, by assumption, nothing is fixed in this vast realm of the possible, so also nothing is ruled out. This condition of a lack of determinacy can be called an *empty infinity*, which is not at all to be confused with an infinite emptiness.

Now man's sense will be stirred, and from the infinite number of possible determinations he will be granted one single actuality. A perception will take shape in him. What had in the prior condition been no more than the empty potential of being open to determination now becomes an effective force, it gains a content; but at the same time, as an effective force, it acquires a limit, since as mere potential it was unlimited. Reality is therefore present, but infinity is lost. To describe a figure in space, we must *limit* infinite space; to imagine a change in time, we must *divide up* temporality. Hence it is only through limits that we can approach reality, only by *negation* or exclusion that we achieve *position* or actual affirmation, only through the surrender of freedom of definition that we can define.

Nonetheless, in all eternity mere exclusion would make no reality, nor would in all eternity a mere sensation become a perception, if there were not *something* to be excluded *from*, if an absolute operation of the mind did not relate negation to something positive, non-affirmation becoming a definite positioning. This activity of the mind is called judging or thinking, and its result is called *thought*.

Before we define a place in space, there is no such thing as space for us; but without the existence of absolute space we would never ever be able to define a place. It is just the same with time. Before we have the moment, we have no sense of temporality; without the existence of eternal time we would never have an idea of the moment. And so it is only through the part that we have access to the whole, only through the limited that we have access to the unlimited, only through passivity that we have access to activity; but it is only through the whole that we have access to the part, only through the unlimited do we have access to the limited, only through activity do we have access to passivity.

If, therefore, it is said of the beautiful that it provides man with a pathway from feeling to thinking, this should not be taken tó mean that the beautiful might bridge the gulf separating feeling from thought, passivity from activity; this gulf is infinite, and without the intervention of a new and autonomous faculty the particular cannot in eternity become universal, the contingent cannot become necessary, the momentary cannot become permanent. The idea is the direct action of this absolute faculty; while it has to be prompted to express itself by the senses, it is in its expression so little dependent upon sensibility that it manifests itself through its opposition to the same. The autonomy of its action excludes any external causation, and so beauty does not *assist* in thinking (which would involve a flagrant contradiction). Only insofar as beauty creates the freedom for powers of thought to express themselves in conformity with its own laws can beauty become a means of leading man from matter to form, from sensations to regularities, from a limited to an absolute existence.

But this presupposes that freedom of the powers of thought could be inhibited, and this seems to conflict with the concept of an autonomous faculty. This is a faculty that receives from the external world nothing but the material upon which it works, which can be hindered only through the withdrawal of this material, hence its effects hindered only negatively; and it would be to misconstrue the very nature of mind if one attributed to sensuous passions the capacity to positively suppress the freedom of spirit. Of course, there are any number of examples given by experience where the powers of reason seem to diminish as sensuous powers become fiercer, but instead of attributing this intellectual weakness to the strength of affect, one should instead explain the overwhelming sway of affect by that weakness of intellect; for the senses can only represent a force to man if his spirit has neglected, of its own free will, to assert itself forcefully.

If I have sought in making this explanation to meet one objection, it seems I have given rise to another, and salvaged the autonomy of mind only at the cost of its unity. For how can mind *of itself* be at once the motive behind both its inactivity and activity if it is not itself divided, if it is not at odds with itself?

Here we need to remember that we are dealing with a finite, not an infinite, mind. The finite mind is that which can do no other than become active through passivity, can attain the absolute only through limitation, acts and shapes only according to the material it receives. A mind of this kind will therefore combine with the impulse for form or for the absolute an impulse for material or limitations, themselves the conditions without which it could neither have the first impulse, nor satisfy it. Establishing the degree to which two such opposed tendencies can exist in the same being is a task that can baffle a metaphysician, but not a transcendental philosopher. The latter claims no ability to explain the possibility of things, but contents himself with establishing the kind of knowledge that is needed to grasp the possibility of experience. And since experience would be as little possible in the absence of this inward conflict of the soul as it would be without its absolute unity, so he has every right to posit both concepts as equally necessary conditions of experience, without worrying himself any further about how they might be reconciled. Naturally, the immanence of these two basic impulses in no sense contradicts the absolute unity of mind, so long as the mind *itself* is distinguished from both impulses. Both impulses exist and have effects *in it*, but the mind is itself neither matter nor form, neither sensibility nor reason; which fact does not always seem to have been considered by those who allow the human mind to act only where it coincides with reason, and declare it to be passive where it contradicts reason.

Each of these fundamental impulses, once developed, necessarily seeks its own satisfaction; since, however, both are necessary, but seek contradictory objects, these dual compulsions cancel each other out, and the will has complete freedom of choice between them. It is therefore the will that relates to both impulses as a *power* (which is the basis of reality), while neither of the two impulses can act of themselves as a power against the other. The most positive impulsion to justice, in which he is by no means wanting, will not prevent a violent man from doing wrong, nor will the most tempting pleasure lead the strong-willed person to break with his principles. There is no power in man other than his will, and he can be robbed of his inner liberty only by that which robs him of his existence: death and all loss of consciousness.

It therefore all depends on the will whether it is the sensuous or the formal impulse which is to be satisfied. But we should mark well: it is not the fact that we feel, but that sensation becomes decisive – not that we achieve self-consciousness, but that the will dictates the way that pure self-ness becomes determinant. The will does not express itself before impulses have had their effect; and these impulses are first aroused when both objects, sensation and self-consciousness, are given. Both must be present before the will can express itself, and so the presence of sensation and self-consciousness cannot be consequent upon will.

A necessity *external to us* determines our condition: our existence in time mediated by sense impressions. This necessity is entirely mechanical and we suffer them to work upon us. And in this same way a necessity *within us* opens up our personality, prompted by those sense impressions and in opposition to them; for self-consciousness cannot depend upon a will that presupposes it. This original manifestation of personality is not our merit, nor is the lack of it our fault. Only someone conscious of himself can demand reason – can demand absolute consistency and universality of consciousness; beforehand he is not man, and no act of humanity can be expected of him. Just as the *metaphysician* cannot explain the limitations imposed upon a free and independent mind by sensation, so the *physicist* cannot understand the infinity which, prompted by these limitations, manifests itself within the personality. Neither abstraction nor experience leads us back to the source from which our concepts of universality and necessity derive; their early appearance hides it from the empirical observer, and their super-sensuous origin hides them from the metaphysical inquirer. But it is enough that self-consciousness exists and, together with its immutable unity, the law of unity is established for the recognition of, and action upon, everything that is *for* man, and everything that will come about *through* him. Ineluctable, incorruptible, inconceivable, a *theophany* if there ever was one, the concepts of truth and justice appear in an age of sensation; and without anyone knowing from what and how it arose we notice the eternal in time, and necessity as subsequent to chance. In this way sensation and self-consciousness emerge, both originating just as much beyond our will as they are beyond our comprehension.

If however both are actual, and if man, through the medium of sensation, experiences a particular existence, once he has experienced through self-consciousness his absolute existence, the two basic impulses and their objects are activated. The material impulse is aroused by the experience of life (with the initiation of individuality), the rational impulse is aroused by the experience of law (with the initiation of personality); now, for the first time, with both in existence, his humanity is constructed. Until this occurs everything happens according to the law of necessity; now the hand of *nature* leaves him and it is *his* task to uphold the humanity that these impulses have implanted within him and opened up for him. As soon as two contrasting basic impulses are active within him, so they both lose their compulsion, and the opposition of two necessities lends *freedom* its origin.*

---

* To avoid any misunderstanding I should note that no matter how often I here talk of freedom, I do not mean the kind of freedom that is necessarily a part of man's intelligence, which can neither be given to him nor taken away, but that freedom which is based upon his mixed nature. The fact that a man only acts rationally evidences a freedom of the first order; and the fact that constrained by materiality he acts rationally, and acts materially according to the laws of reason, evidences a freedom of the second order. One could simply explain the latter as a natural possibility of the former.

TWENTIETH LETTER

The very concept of freedom implies its autonomy; but it also follows directly from the foregoing that *freedom is itself* an effect of *nature* (in this word's widest possible sense), and not of man; so it follows from this that freedom can be furthered or inhibited by natural means. It evolves once man is a *complete being*, when *both* of his basic impulses have developed, and it will therefore be absent so long as man is incomplete and excluded from one of his two impulses; and should be capable of restoration by all that returns him to completeness.

Now it is actually possible that we can point to a moment, both in the entire human species and in the individual man, when man is not yet complete and one of the two impulses is exclusively active in him. We know that he begins with nothing but life, so that he might end with form; that he is an individual before becoming a person, that he proceeds from limits to infinity. The material impulse takes effect earlier than the rational impulse, because sensation precedes consciousness, and in this priority of the material impulse we find the key to the entire history of human liberty.

For there is one moment when the life impulse, still free of the counteracting force of the formal impulse, acts as nature and necessity; when sensuousness is a power because man has not yet begun; for in man himself there can be no power other than the will. But quite on the contrary, in the condition of thought into which man should now move, reason should be a power, logical or moral necessity taking the place of physical necessity. The power of sensation has to be destroyed before its law can be established. It is not therefore sufficient that something begins that has not hitherto existed; something that had existed must first come to an end. Man cannot move from sensation to thought directly; he has to take *a step back*, since one determination has to be annulled if its contrary is to take its place. Hence to replace passivity with autonomous activity, to exchange a passive determination for an active one, he must be *momentarily free of any determination*, existing in the condition of simply being open to determination; for if one wishes to move from minus to plus, one has to pass through zero. Consequently, he must in a way return to that negative state in which he lacks all determination, the condition in which he found himself before anything had made any kind of impression on his senses. That condition was completely empty of content; now it is a matter of combining the same absence of definition, and an equally unlimited degree of determinability, with the greatest possible content, since from this situation something positive should result. The definition that he receives through sensation has to be grasped firmly, for he must not lose reality; but this reality, to the extent that it presents a limitation, must at the same time be annulled, because an unlimited availability for definition is to emerge. The task is therefore to both destroy and retain the determination of this condition, which is possible in only one way: by *confronting it with another*. When its pans are empty, a scale balances; but it also balances if the pans contain equal weights.

The soul thus moves from sensation to thought through an intermediate disposition in which sense and reason *are both* active; and for exactly the same reason their determining forces nullify each other, and through their counter-position bring about a negation. This intermediate disposition, where the soul is under neither physical nor moral constraint but is nonetheless active both physically and morally, deserves to be called a free disposition; and if the condition of sensuous determination is called the physical, while the condition of rational determination is called the logical and moral, then this condition of real and active determinability has to be called the *aesthetic.**

---

* Readers who are not entirely familiar with the pure meaning of a word which, through ignorance, has been so very abused, may find the following explanation helpful. All things that can appear as phenomena can be considered in terms of four different relations. A thing can relate directly to our sensible condition (our existence and well-being); that is its physical formation. Or it can relate to our intellect, and provide us with some knowledge; that is its *logical* formation. Or it can relate to our will, and be treated as an object of choice for a rational being; that is its *moral* formation. Or, finally, it can relate to the entirety of our various powers, without being for any one of them a particular object; and that is its *aesthetic* formation. A person can please us by his readiness to do us a service; his conversation can give us something to think about; his character can arouse feelings of admiration; but finally, by our simply looking at him and on the basis of his appearance alone, he can be to our liking; independently of all of the foregoing we might, in judging him, taking no account of any law or any kind of purpose, decide that we just like him. In this last quality we are exercising an aesthetic judgement. Consequently, there is education for health, education for insight, education for morality, and education for taste and beauty. This last aims at the most harmonious development of the whole of our sensuous and intellectual powers. Because one can be seduced by poor taste, and through faulty reasoning be reinforced in this error, the concept of the arbitrary is freely associated with that of the aesthetic; and so I note here somewhat superfluously (although these letters on aesthetic education deal with virtually nothing other than the disproof of this error) that the soul in aesthetic circumstances is certainly free to act, and free to the greatest extent from all compulsion, but it is not free to act independently of the law. Hence this aesthetic liberty can be distinguished from logical necessity in thinking, and moral necessity in desire, only by the fact that the laws to which the soul conforms here *are not presented* and – since they meet no resistance – do not appear to be compulsion.

TWENTY-FIRST LETTER

As I remarked at the beginning of the last letter,[1] there is a dual condition of determinability, and a dual condition of determination. I can now clarify this proposition.

The soul can be determined, but only if it is not yet determined; but it can also be determined if it is not determined in such a way as to exclude anything; hence while being determined it remains unlimited. The first is merely lack of determination (it lacks bounds because it lacks reality); the second is the capacity for aesthetic determination (it has no bounds, because it unites all reality).

The soul is determined if it has any kind of restriction; but it is also determined if it restricts itself by means of its own absolute faculty. It finds itself in the first condition if it feels, and in the second if it thinks. And so thinking, in regard to determination, is complementary to the aesthetic disposition with respect to determinability; the former is restriction by virtue of its inner infinite force, the latter is negation by virtue of inner infinite abundance. Just as sensation and thinking coincide at one single point, such that for both sensation and thinking the soul determines that man is something (either individual or person) to the exclusion of all else, otherwise being poles apart; so in the same way aesthetic determinability coincides with mere lack of determination at the one point where both exclude all determinate existence, while at all other points they are infinitely varied, all or nothing. If the latter, the lack of determinability is imagined as an *empty infinity*, so the aesthetic freedom to determine, which is its real counterpart, has to be treated as a *fulfilled infinity*:

something that coincides most exactly with the foregoing inquiry.[2]

In the aesthetic state man is therefore a *nullity*, if one takes account of any particular resultant and not of his entire capacity, and if the lack of any particular determination in him is at issue. Some declare that the beautiful and the mood that it arouses within our soul are, in respect of *knowledge* and *conviction*, without merit and so a matter of indifference; and in this we would have to concede that they are completely right. They are completely right, because beauty provides no single result for either intellect or will; it follows neither one single intellectual aim, nor any one moral purpose; it discovers not one truth, does not help us fulfil any special duty; in sum, it is as unsuitable for the foundation of character as it is for enlightening one's brain. Beauty is *nature*, and man owes both its concepts and its resolutions only *to himself*. In aesthetic culture the personal worth of a man, or his dignity insofar is this is something that lies within his power, remains completely undetermined; and no more is achieved other than the fact that, *thanks to nature*, he can henceforth make of himself what he will – that the liberty of being what he ought to be is fully restored to him.

But in just this way something infinite is achieved. For as soon as we recall that this liberty was taken from him by the unilateral compulsion of nature in the realm of sensation, and the exclusive legislation of reason in the realm of thought, then we have to admit that the capacity which the aesthetic disposition restores to him is the highest of all bounties: the bounty of humanity. Of course, he is already endowed with the potential of this humanity before each particular condition which he attains; but in practice he loses it with every particular condition of which he makes use. And so this humanity has to be restored to him each time anew through the aesthetic life, if he is to be able to pass into an opposite condition.*

---

* It is true that the rapidity with which certain characters pass from sensations to thoughts, or to decisions, renders the aesthetic disposition that they must necessarily pass through hardly noticeable. Souls of this kind cannot long withstand the condition of indeterminacy and press impatiently for a result that they cannot find in the condition of aesthetic limitlessness. By contrast,

It is not then merely poetically permissible, but also phil-osophically proper, to call beauty our second creator. For whether beauty simply makes humanity a possibility for us, leaving to our own free will any decision about how far we wish to actualize this, it shares in common with our original creator, nature, which likewise did no more than offer the capacity for humanity, the fact that any use of this potentiality is left to a decision made by our own free will.

---

among others, who seek their pleasure more in the feeling of *total capacity* than in any single action, the aesthetic condition spreads itself over a much greater area. As much as the former fear emptiness, the latter can as little bear limitation. I hardly need to remind you that the former are born for detail and subordinate affairs, while the latter, supposing that they combine this capacity with a sense of reality, are destined for the whole, and for great roles.

TWENTY-SECOND LETTER

If the aesthetic disposition of the soul has in one respect to be treated as a *nullity* just as soon as one's attention is turned to individual and particular effects, in other respects it is to be regarded as a condition of *supreme reality*, given the absence of all barriers and the sum of the powers jointly active within it. One cannot therefore say that those who regard the aesthetic condition as the most fruitful in respect of knowledge and morality are entirely wrong. They are in fact completely right, for a disposition of the soul that comprehends all of humanity must necessarily and potentially also include within it every individual expression; a disposition of the soul that removes all limits from the entirety of human nature must necessarily also remove these limits from every single expression of the same. And for exactly this reason, that it provides exclusive protection to no one individual function of humanity, so it is favourable to one and all without discrimination, and it confers advantage on no individual because it is the foundation of possibility for all. Every other operation confers upon the soul a special skill, but for doing so sets a particular limit; only the aesthetic leads to the state of unlimitedness. Every other condition into which we can enter refers us back to a prior one, and for its termination requires a following one; only the aesthetic is a totality in itself, uniting in itself all the conditions of its origin and of its persistence. Only here do we feel ourselves torn from time; and our humanity expresses itself with a purity and *integrity* as if it had still not suffered any impairment from the impact of external forces.

Our senses are caressed by direct sensation, opening up our susceptible and mobile soul to each and every impression; but this does at the same time make us less capable of any exertion. Whatever stresses our powers of thought and prompts the development of abstruse concepts strengthens our mind and readies it for any kind of resistance; but this strengthening also hardens it, losing in receptivity as much as is gained for autonomous action. For this reason both the one and the other ultimately and necessarily lead to exhaustion, since material cannot long go without creative power, nor can such power long go without creative material. If by contrast we have given ourselves the enjoyment of true beauty, at such a moment we are master equally of our passive and active powers; and with the same facility we will turn to seriousness and to play, to rest and to movement, to compliance and to resistance, to abstract thought and to intuition.

This high level of equanimity and freedom of the mind, linked to power and vigour, is the mood in which a genuine work of art should leave us; there is no more certain touchstone of authentic aesthetic quality. If after an enjoyment of this kind we find ourselves disposed to prefer one particular way of feeling or of acting, while being unfitted for or disinclined to another, this serves as unmistakable proof that we have not experienced a *purely aesthetic* effect, whether this results from the object itself, our mode of response or (as is nearly always the case) from both together.

Since in reality we can encounter no purely aesthetic effect (since man can never escape a dependence on his powers), the sublimity of a work of art can only consist in its close approximation to that ideal of aesthetic purity; and however close we might allow that approximation to be, we will always move on in a particular mood, and with our own thoughts. The more universal the mood, and the less limited the thoughts that a particular kind of art and its particular effects arouse in our soul, the more refined that kind of art, and so the more sublime is its product. This can be tested with works from the different arts, and with different works from the same kind of art. A piece of fine music leaves us with the sense that our feelings have been aroused; a fine piece of poetry enlivens our imagination; a fine painting or building stirs our understanding. If directly following a sublime musical experience someone seeks to engage us with abstruse ideas; immediately following a sublime poetic experience seeks to involve us in routine everyday business; immediately following our contemplation of fine painting and sculpture seeks to inflame our powers of imagination and ambush our feelings – this person would have chosen his time badly. The reason for this is that even the most inspired music, *by virtue of its materiality*, has a greater affinity with our senses than true aesthetic freedom permits; even the most successful poem partakes more of the coincidental and accidental play of imagination, *as its medium*, than the inner necessity of the truly beautiful admits; even the most sublime sculpture (and this perhaps most of all) borders upon rigorous science *by virtue of its conceptual precision*. These special affinities diminish as the attainment of a work from these three kinds of art increases; and it is a necessary and natural consequence of their perfection that, without any change to their objective bounds, the various arts become ever more similar to each other *in their impact upon the soul*. In its highest refinement music has to become form, working upon us with the serene power of Antiquity; the plastic arts must, in their highest perfection, become music and move us by their directly sensuous presence; poetry in its most complete development must seize us as music does, but also like the plastic arts envelop us with serene clarity. This marks the perfection of style in every art: that it is able to remove its own limits without annulling its own specific properties, and by prudent use of its particular nature lend it a general character.

The work of the artist must overcome not only the limitations that the specific character of his art involves, but also those presented by the particular material with which he works. In a genuinely fine work of art the content should do nothing, the form everything; for it is form alone that has an impact on the whole man, while content affects only his individual powers. However exalted and comprehensive the content may be, it always has a limiting effect on the mind, and true aesthetic freedom is to be expected only from the form. This is the real artistic secret of the master, *that he erases material with form*; the more imposing, presumptuous, seductive is the material in itself, the more decisively it seeks to impose *its own* effect, or the more the observer is disposed to become directly involved with the material, then the more triumphant the art that forces it back and asserts its rule. The soul of the observer and of the listener must remain completely free and intact; the magic of the artist must leave it as pure and complete as would the hands of the Creator. The most frivolous subject must be treated in such a way that we can move directly on to the most austere seriousness. The most serious material must be treated in such a way that we retain the ability to exchange it for the most transient playfulness. Arts of affect, as with tragedy, are no objection: for *in the first place*, they are not completely free arts, since they are in the service of a particular purpose (of pathos); and *then* no person truly acquainted with the arts would deny that works, even those of this class, are all the more perfect the more that they shield the liberty of the soul, even in the course of the most violent emotional storms. There is indeed a fine art of passion; but a fine passionate art is a contradiction, for the unfailing effect of the beautiful is freedom from passions. No less contradictory is the concept of a fine pedagogic (didactic) or improving (moral) art, since nothing conflicts with the concept of beauty more than ascribing a specific tendency to the soul.

If a work makes an impact purely by virtue of its content, this is not always proof of its formlessness; it can just as often be testimony to a lack of form in the person judging. If he is either too tensed or too relaxed, if he is used to relying exclusively on either his understanding or his senses for what he apprehends, he will only ever appreciate the parts of the best-realized whole, and notice only the material used in the most beautiful form. Receptive only to a basic *element*, he first has to destroy the aesthetic organization of a work before he can find pleasure in it, scratching carefully away at the individual detail which the artist, with infinite skill, had submerged in the harmony of the whole. His interest in it is either moral or material;

whatever it might be, it is not what it should be: aesthetic. Such readers enjoy a serious and moving poem as if it were a sermon, and a simple and humorous poem like an intoxicating drink; and if they were sufficiently tasteless to demand *edification* of a tragedy or an epic, even if it were about the Messiah,[1] they certainly would not fail to take exception to a song in the manner of Anacreon or Catullus.[2]

TWENTY-THIRD LETTER

I resume once more the thread of my inquiry, having broken off only so that I might apply the principles I have advanced to the practice of art and the judgement of its works.

The transition from the passive state of sensation to active thinking and willing occurs in no other way than through an intermediate state of aesthetic freedom; and although this condition decides nothing either for our insight or for our conviction, and also leaves our intellectual and moral value quite problematic, it is all the same the necessary precondition by which we alone can attain insight and conviction. In sum: there is no other way of making the sensuous man rational than by first making him aesthetic.

But you will want to object: is this mediation really indispensable? Should not truth and duty, of and by themselves, be able to find a way into the sensuous man? To which I must answer: not only can they, they should indeed owe their determining power only to themselves; nothing would be more contradictory to my earlier assertions than if they would seem to advocate the opposite opinion. It has been expressly proved that beauty provides no resultant, either for the intellect or for the will; that it in no way becomes involved with thinking and decision-making; that it rather provides us with the capacity for both, but has nothing to do at all with the actual use of this capacity. Here all outside assistance is excluded, and the pure logical form, the concept, must relate directly to the intellect, and the pure moral form, the law, directly to the will.

But the fact that it can do this at all – that any pure form can exist for the sensuous man – I claim that this must first be made possible by the aesthetic disposition of the soul. Truth is not something that can, like actuality or the physical existence of things, simply be received from elsewhere; it is something freely created by the power of thought itself; and this autonomy, this freedom, is exactly what we miss in the sensuous man. The sensuous man is already (physically) determined, and so as a result has no scope for further determination; he must necessarily first regain what has here been lost before he can exchange his passive determination for an active one. But he cannot receive this back except by losing the passive determination which he had, or *by already possessing within himself the active determination* to which he should proceed. If he only lost the passive determination, then he would at the same time lose the possibility of active determination; for thought needs a body, and form can only be realized in material of some kind. He will therefore have to have the latter already within himself, he will have to be determined both passively and actively at the same time: which means he will have to become aesthetic.

Through the aestheticization of the soul, the autonomy of reason is opened to the domain of sensibility, the power of sensation broken even within its own boundaries, and the physical man refined to such an extent that henceforth spiritual man only needs to develop himself from the physical according to the laws of freedom. The step from the aesthetic condition to the logical and moral condition (from beauty to truth and duty) is thus infinitely easier than the step from the physical state to the aesthetic (from mere blind life to form). Man can simply make the former step by his own free will, since it involves only taking, not giving, only fragmenting his nature, not enlarging it; the aestheticized man will make universally valid judgements, and act in a universally valid way, as soon as he wants to. Nature must make it easier for him to make the step from raw matter to beauty, in which an entirely new form of activity is to be opened up in him; and his will cannot exert any influence over a disposition that itself first lent the will existence. To lead the aesthetic man to insight and lofty convictions one can do no more than give him strong incentives; and to get that from the sensuous man one first has to change his nature. Aesthetic man often needs no more than the challenge of an exalted situation (which works directly upon his willpower) to make him a hero and a wise man; sensuous man has on the other hand first to be transposed under another sky.

One of the most important tasks of culture is thus to subordinate man to form even in his purely physical life and render him aesthetic insofar as the realm of beauty can reach him; for it is only from the aesthetic condition, and not from the physical, that the moral condition can develop. If man is in every particular case to possess the ability to make his own judgement and will the judgement of the human species, if he is to find from that restricted existence a path to an infinite one, and be able from that dependent condition to take flight into independence and liberty – then we must see to it that he is at no point simply an individual serving natural laws. If he is capable of and ready for lifting himself from the closed circle of natural ends to the embracing of rational ends, then he must already *within the first* be practised for the second, already have realized his physical destiny with a certain freedom of spirit, in accordance with the laws of beauty.

And he can do this, without in the least contradicting his physical purpose. The claims of nature on him relate only to *what he does, the content* of his action; on the way *in which* he does it, the form of it – natural ends define nothing here. By contrast, the claims of reason are rigorously directed to the form of his activity. However necessary it might be for his moral determination that he be purely moral, that he demonstrates absolute autonomy, for his physical determination it is a matter of complete indifference whether he is purely physical, or whether he behaves in a purely passive manner. Regarding the latter, it is a matter entirely in his own discretion whether he presents himself merely as a sensuous being, as a natural force (as a force that acts only as it is acted upon), or whether at the same time he presents himself as an absolute force, as a rational being; and there should be no question about which of the two is more fitting to his dignity. Rather, the more that it debases and degrades him to do from sensuous motives that which he should have decided to do from pure motives of duty, the more it honours and ennobles him to strive for regularity, harmony and lack of all restriction even where the common man is content to quench his permitted desires.* In sum: where

* This inspired and aesthetically free treatment of common reality is, wherever one encounters it, the sign of a *refined* soul. A refined soul is in general one with the gift of transforming the most limited task and the most petty object into something infinite by the way in which it is handled. Refined is every form that leaves the mark of autonomy on anything that, by its nature, merely *serves* something else (is merely a means). A refined spirit is not content to be free itself, but has to set everything around it free as well, even those things that are lifeless. Beauty is, however, the sole possible phenomenal expression of liberty. The prevailing expression of *intelligence* in a face or a work of art can therefore never be refined, in the same way that it can never be beautiful, because it emphasizes, rather than conceals, a dependence that is itself inseparable from purposefulness.

The moral philosopher does teach us that man can never do *more* than his duty, merely meaning by that the relationship that actions can have to the moral law. But for actions that relate to just one particular purpose, to *exceed this purpose* in the realm of the super-sensuous (which here can mean nothing other than to fulfil the physical in an aesthetic manner) means at the same time *to exceed duty*, in that this can only prescribe that the *will* is sacred, not that *nature* has itself assumed a sacred quality. There is thus no moral transcendence of duty, but there is an aesthetic transcendence, and such conduct is called refined. With refined conduct there is always an element of supererogation that possesses a free and formal value despite needing only a material value, or combined with the inner value that it should possess another external value that it could do without; and many have for this reason taken aesthetic supererogation for a moral one and, seduced by the appearance of the refined, themselves implanted arbitrariness and chance into morality which would end in its complete annulment.

Refined conduct is to be distinguished from sublime conduct. The first transcends moral obligation, but not the latter, even though we regard it much more highly than the former. We do not esteem it because it transcends the rational concept of its object (the moral law), but because it transcends the empirical concept of its subject (our knowledge of the qualities of human will and of its strength); on the other hand, we do not esteem refined conduct because it surpasses the nature of its subject, from which it should rather flow freely and without constraint, but because it moves beyond the nature of its object (physical purpose) into the realm of the spirit. There, one would like to say, we marvel at the victory that the object achieves over man; here, we admire the impetus that man gives to the object.

the formal impulse should rule, in the domain of truth and morality, there can be no matter, sensation determines nothing; but where the material impulse rules, in the domain of happiness and well-being, form has every right to exist, and the playful impulse to command.

And so here, upon the indifferent field of physical life, man must begin his moral life; while still passive he must become autonomous and active, even in his sensuous limits he must initiate his freedom to reason. He must even submit his inclinations to the law of his will; he must, if you will permit me the expression, wage war against matter on its own ground, so that he might be spared having to fight this fearful foe on the holy ground of liberty. He must learn to have *more noble* desires, so that he does not find it necessary *to wish to be sublime*. This will be effected by aesthetic culture, which subordinates to the laws of beauty everything that neither the natural laws of human caprice, nor laws of reason can comprehend; and in the form that it lends to the outer life, already opens the way to the inner life.

TWENTY-FOURTH LETTER

Hence there are three different moments, or stages, of development to be distinguished through which both the individual man as well as the entire species must necessarily pass in a particular order if they are to fulfil the entire arc of their destiny. Chance causes, stemming from the influence of external circumstance or the whim of man, can either prolong or cut short particular periods; but none can be completely omitted, and the order in which they succeed one another cannot be reversed either by nature or by human will. In his *physical* condition man suffers merely the force of nature; he detaches himself from this power in the *aesthetic* condition, and prevails over it in the *moral* condition.

What is man before beauty coaxes from him unbridled pleasure for its own sake, and the serenity of form tempers his wild life? Eternally uniform in his aims, eternally capricious in his judgements, self-obsessed without ever being properly himself, footloose without being free, a slave without a rule to follow. During this era the world is for him mere fate, not yet an object for itself; everything exists for him only insofar as it lends him existence; what neither gives to him, nor takes from him, simply does not exist for him. Any phenomenon that he encounters is isolated and detached, as he is himself in the chain of being. Everything that exists for him is only by virtue of the passing moment, every change is for him an entirely novel creation, since with the lack of necessity *in himself* there is also a lack of any necessity *beyond himself* that could connect ever-changing shapes into a universe which, given that the individual is fleeting, could lock down these shifting features with unvarying law. In vain does nature's rich variety pass before his senses; he sees in its wonderful profusion nothing but his own booty, in its power and greatness nothing but his foe. Either he hurls himself upon things to devour them greedily, or things threaten to destroy him and he bats them away in horror. In both cases his relation to the sensuous world is one of immediate *contact*; and forever distressed by the way that it presses upon him, unceasingly tortured by peremptory desire, he finds tranquillity only in fatigue, and no boundaries other than in exhausted desire.

> The Titan's mighty breast and nervous frame
> Was his descendants' certain heritage;
> But round their brow Jove forg'd a band of brass.
> Wisdom and patience, prudence and restraint,
> He from their gloomy, fearful eye conceal'd;
> In them each passion grew to savage rage,
> And headlong rush'd uncheck'd.
>
> Goethe, *Iphigenia in Tauris*[1]

Unfamiliar with *his own* human dignity, he is far from honouring it in others; and, conscious of his own savage greed, he fears it in each creature that seems like him. He never sees others in himself, only himself in others; and society, instead of rendering him part of a species, locks him ever more closely into his individuality. Blinkered in this way he wanders aimlessly through his benighted life until a benevolent nature unburdens his clouded senses, distinguishes the reflection *of himself* from things that now stand revealed in the reflected light of his consciousness.

Of course, the raw state of nature presented here cannot be shown to have existed among any particular people, or at any one time; it is merely an idea, but an idea that in certain respects coincides with experience most exactly. It can be said that man never was in this brutish condition, but neither has he entirely escaped from it. Unmistakable traces of freedom of thought can be found even in the rawest subjects, just as in the most cultivated there is no shortage of moments recalling that dismal state of nature. Man is unique in combining both the highest and the lowest in his nature, and if his *dignity* derives from a strict distinction of the one from the other, his *happiness* depends upon its skilful supersession. Culture, which should harmonize his worth and his happiness, will therefore have to ensure the utmost purity of these two principles even while they are most closely combined.

The first sign of reason in man is thus not yet the beginning of his humanity. This last is first decided by his freedom. And reason begins only then to render his sensuous dependence without limit; a phenomenon whose importance and generality has not, it seems to me, been appropriately developed. We know that reason can be recognized in man through the demand for an absolute that is founded upon itself and is necessary; and since this cannot be adequately met in any isolated state of his physical life, this demand compels him to leave physical life completely and move on from a limited reality to ideas. But although the true meaning of that demand is to tear him away from the bonds of time and lead him from a sensuous world into an ideal world, it can instead – thanks to a misapprehension then hard to avoid, given the all-pervasive sensuousity of the time – direct itself to physical life, and so, instead of rendering man independent, he is plunged into the most terrible servitude.

And so this is what actually happens. Born aloft on the wings of the power of imagination, man leaves behind the close confines of the present, which includes simple animality, so that he might seek the unlimited future that lies before him; but while infinity opens up before his giddy *imagination*, his heart has not yet ceased to live in the individual, serving the moment. This impulse to the absolute has taken him by surprise in all his animality – and since in this dulled state all his efforts are directed simply to the material and the temporal, restricted by his own individuality, he is therefore merely prompted by this imperative to lend his individuality infinite extension, rather than abstract from it; instead of striving for form, he strives for an endless source of material; instead of striving for something unchanging, he strives for eternal change, and an absolute assurance of his temporal existence. This impulse which, when applied to his thought and action, should lead to truth and morality, now when applied to his present passivity and feeling brings nothing but unlimited yearning, and absolute need. The first fruits that he reaps in the realm of the spirit are therefore *trouble* and *fear*; both are the outcome of reason, not of sensuousness, but a reason that misses its mark and applies its imperative directly to matter. The fruits from this tree are all dogmatic eudaemonian systems lacking in any specificity that might fit them to the present day, or an entire life;[2] or, something which renders them no more respectable, all eternity. A limitless time of being and well-being purely for the sake of existence and of well-being is merely an ideal expressing a yearning; a demand whose striving for the absolute is purely animalistic. Hence, without gaining something for his humanity through such manifestations of reason, man in this way merely forfeits the contented and limited state of the animal, over whom he now enjoys only the unenviable advantage of losing possession of the present in seeking a future, without ever having sought anything other than his present in these entirely limitless vistas.

But if reason does not miss its mark, its object, and does not err in posing its question, sensuousness will for a considerable time falsify the answer. As soon as man has begun to use his reason and connect causes and purposes in the phenomena he encounters, reason applies its concepts and insists on both an absolute connection and an unconditional cause. To simply raise such a demand man must already have gone beyond sensuousness; but sensuousness makes use of exactly this demand to recover the truant. This would be the point where he would entirely depart from the sensuous world and soar into the realm of ideas; for intellect remains eternally within the terms of what is determined, and inquires eternally, without ever coming to a conclusion. But here we are talking about man, and he is not yet capable of such an abstraction; what he does not find in his *sphere of empirical knowledge*, beyond which he does not yet seek for pure reason, he will seek below that in his *sphere of feeling* and, apparently, find it. Of course, sensuousness does not show him anything that could be his own cause, and which might of itself provide law; but it does show him something that knows of no cause, and which recognizes no law. Since he is unable to calm his questioning intellect with any ultimate and inner cause, he at least silences that intellect by resorting to the concept of *that which has no cause*, remaining within the blind coercion of matter, since he is not yet capable of grasping the sublime necessity of reason. Since sensuousness knows of no *purpose* other than its own advantage, and feels itself to be impelled by no *cause* other than blind chance, so he allows the former to dictate his actions, and the latter to be the ruler of the world.

Even the moral law, that which is most sacred in man, cannot evade this falsification when it first appears in sensuousness. Since it only expresses itself in prohibitions, opposing the interest of his self-love, this moral law must seem something alien so long as he has not yet perceived that this very self-love is alien, and the voice of reason his true self. He senses only the fetters that reason lays upon him, and not the unending liberation that it gives him. Without appreciating the inherent worth of the legislator, he feels only the coercion and impotent resistance of the subject. Since in his experience the material impulse *precedes* the moral impulse, he also ascribes to the law of necessity an origin in time, a *positive origin*, and by the most unfortunate of all errors makes what is unchanging and essentially eternal an accidental outcome of the transient. He persuades himself that the concepts of right and wrong are statutes that have been deliberately introduced, not as concepts that of themselves are valid for all time. Just as in the explanation of individual natural phenomena he goes beyond *nature* and looks there for what can only be found in its inner regularity, so in explaining the moral sphere he goes beyond *reason*, and forfeits his humanity by seeking in this way a deity. No wonder that a religion purchased with the disposal of his humanity seems worthy of such a derivation if he considers laws that were not binding *from* all eternity are also not binding unconditionally *in* all eternity. He is not involved with a holy being, but merely with a powerful one. The spirit in which he worships his god is therefore fear, which humiliates him; not reverence, which raises him in his own estimation.

Although these multifarious deviations of man from the ideal of his destiny could not have all occurred at that time – there being many stations on the way from thoughtlessness to error, from lack of will to the corruption of will – they do all follow from his physical condition, for in everything the impulse to life trumps the formal impulse. It may be that reason in man has not yet expressed itself in any way, and the physical still rules over him with blind necessity; or that reason has not yet purged itself from the senses sufficiently, and the moral continues to be at the service of the physical; no matter, in both cases he is entirely swayed by material principle, and man is, ultimately at least, a sensuous being; the sole difference being that in the first case he is an animal lacking reason, and in the second a reasoning animal. But he should be neither of these; he should be a man; he should not be ruled by nature exclusively, nor should reason rule him conditionally. Both of these systems should remain entirely independent of each other, and yet be perfectly as one.

TWENTY-FIFTH LETTER

So long as man in his initial physical condition responds only passively to the sensuous world, simply by feeling, he is still completely at one with it; and because he is himself just part of the world, there is as yet no world for him. It is only when he is in his aesthetic condition, standing apart from himself or *observing* himself, that his personality detaches itself from this world; and because he has now ceased to identify himself with that world, it is now evident to him.*

Contemplation (reflection) is the first liberal relation of man to the universe which surrounds him. If desire seizes its object directly, contemplation shifts its own object into the distance, and by doing so makes this object its true and inalienable property, putting it beyond all passion. Once man begins to contemplate, the necessity of nature that had ruled him with undivided force in the condition of mere sensation begins to weaken; in his senses there is a momentary calm; time itself, eternally changing, stands still; the scattered rays of consciousness draw

---

* I emphasize once more that, while both of these periods must necessarily be separated in the idea, they become more or less mixed together in experience. Nor must one think that there was once a time when man found himself solely in this physical situation, and a time when he had entirely detached himself from it. Once man *perceives an object in the world separate from himself he is no longer in a merely physical condition*; and so long as he continues perceiving such an object he will not escape this physical condition, since he can only see it, hence sense it. The three moments that I listed at the beginning of the Twenty-fourth Letter are on the whole three different eras in the development of the whole of humanity, and for the entire development of one single man; but they can also be distinguished in every single perception of an object, and so are in sum the necessary conditions for all knowledge received through our senses.

together, and an image of the infinite – as *form* – is reflected in transience. Once light glimmers in man he is no longer benighted; as soon as he grows still the storm in the universe abates, and the clashing forces of nature find a calm within lasting boundaries. It is thus no wonder that the ancient sagas talk of this great event within man as if it were a revolution in the external world, and sensuousize the thought that triumphs over the laws of time in the image of a Zeus who put an end to the reign of Saturn.[1]

Man was a slave to nature as long as he merely felt it; he became its sovereign once he began to think it. What had previously ruled over him as *force* is now the *object* of his judging gaze. What to him is an object has no power over him; for to be an object it must be subject to his own power. Insofar as he lends form to matter, and so long as there is matter, he is invulnerable to its effects; for nothing can harm a spirit except that which takes his liberty, and he proves his own liberty by giving form to the formless. Fear only has a place where ponderous and shapeless mass rules, its indistinct outlines shifting between insecure boundaries; man has the advantage over any terror in nature once he knows how to lend it form, and transform it into his object. In the same way that he begins to maintain his independence against phenomenal nature, he also maintains his worth against nature as a power, and with noble liberty rises up against his gods. They throw off the spectral masks with which they had made his childhood so anxious, and surprise him with his own image, for they turn into his own projection. The divine monster of Orientals that bestrode the world with the blind force of the predator, shrinks in Greek imagination into the friendly shape of mankind; the empire of Titans collapses, and infinite force is restrained by infinite form.

Even though I only sought a way out of the material world and entry to the world of spirit, my unconstrained power of imagination has already led me into the heart of the latter. The beauty that we seek is already behind us, and we have skipped over it by moving directly from mere life to pure form and to pure object. But a leap of this kind is not in human nature, and to keep abreast of this nature we will need to return again to the sensuous world.

Beauty is, of course, the work of free contemplation, and with it we enter the world of ideas; but it must be noted that in so doing we do not quit the sensuous world, as happens with knowledge of the truth. This is the pure outcome of abstracting from everything that is material and contingent; a pure object in which no restriction of the subject might remain, pure autonomous activity without a trace of passivity. There is, of course, a way back to sensuousness from the highest level of abstraction, since thought touches inner sensations, and the idea of logical and moral unity transmutes into a feeling of sensuous concurrence. But when we divert ourselves with knowledge, then we make a very exact distinction between our imagination and our sensation, treating the latter as something contingent that could be omitted without knowledge ceasing, and without truth not being truth. This remains what it is, even if it prompts no passion in the senses, even if there were no senses, and in the concept of divinity we simply allow truth to remain, and all sensuousness to cease. It would, however, be a quite vain undertaking to seek the separation of this relationship to our capacity to feel from the idea of *beauty*; and so we do treat the one as an effect of the other, but must regard both at once and reciprocally as effect and as cause. In our pleasure in knowledge we have no trouble in distinguishing the *transition* from activity to passivity, and clearly notice that the first is over if the latter begins. By contrast, with our pleasure in beauty no such successive distinction can be made between activity and passivity, and here reflection flows so completely into feeling that we believe ourselves to be directly apprehending form. Beauty is thus an *object* for us, for reflection is the condition for any sensation of it that we may have; but at the same time beauty is a *state of our subject*, since feeling is the condition according to which we form an idea of it. Beauty is therefore certainly form, since we observe it; but it is at the same time life, because we feel it. In a word: beauty is at once our situation and our deed.

And just because it is at once both, so beauty serves us with triumphant proof that passivity by no means precludes activity, nor matter form, nor limitation infinity – hence that the necessarily physical dependency of man in no respect abrogates his moral freedom. Beauty proves this, and I must add, it *alone* can prove this to us. For in the enjoyment of truth or of logical unity feeling does not necessarily coincide with thought, but rather follows on from it coincidentally. This can merely prove to us that a sensuous nature can follow from a rational one, and vice versa; not that they coexist, nor that they affect each other reciprocally, nor that they can be absolutely and necessarily united. Quite the contrary: from this exclusion of feeling so long as we think, and of thinking so long as we feel, we might even conclude that these two natures are *irreconcilable*; and in fact analytical philosophers know of no better proof for the realizability of pure reason in mankind than that it has to be so. But since the enjoyment of beauty or of *aesthetic unity* presupposes a real *union* and transposition of matter with form, and of passivity with activity, the *possibility of uniting* both natures, the realization of the infinite in the finite (including the possibility of the most sublime humanity), is proved in exactly this way.

We should therefore no longer feel at a loss in finding a transition from sensuous dependency to moral freedom once beauty has shown how this is possible: that the latter is entirely compatible with the former; and that man does not need to flee matter to prove himself as spirit. But if he is already free while associated with sensuousness, as the fact of beauty teaches; and if freedom is something absolute and super-sensuous, as is necessarily implied by its concept; then it can no longer be a question of how he might achieve the movement from limitation to the absolute, how in his thinking and wanting he might set himself against sensuousness, since this has already happened with beauty. In short, it can no longer be a question of how he passes from beauty to a truth already potentially implied in beauty; but instead, how he opens up a path for himself from a common reality to an aesthetic reality – how he moves from mere feelings of ordinary life to feelings of beauty.

TWENTY-SIXTH LETTER

As I have argued in the preceding letters, since it is the aesthetic mood of the soul that first gives rise to liberty, it can be easily seen that it cannot originate in liberty, and can consequently have no moral origin. It has to be a gift of nature; only the favour of chance can loosen the fetters of the original physical condition, and lead the savage to beauty.[1]

The germ of beauty will develop very little where a meagre nature denies man all invigoration, and where a wasteful nature relieves him of any effort – where dull sensuousness feels no need, and where powerful appetite finds no satisfaction. Certainly not where man skulks in caves *like a troglodyte*, eternally alone, never finding mankind *beyond himself*; nor where he roams *nomadically* in vast hordes, eternally a mere number, never finding mankind *in himself*. His tender beauty will bud only when he sits alone in his hut in quiet contemplation of himself and, when he leaves his hut, talks to all of his kind. There, where a gentle ether opens the senses to every delicate touch, and luxuriant matter is imbued with energy and warmth – where the dominion of blind mass even in lifeless creation has been overthrown, and triumphant form ennobles even the lowest nature – there, in those joyful surroundings and in that hallowed zone where only activity leads to pleasure, and pleasure to activity, where from life itself divine order flows, and from the law of order only life develops, where the power of imagination eternally flees reality, yet never strays from the simplicity of nature: here alone will sense and spirit, receptive and formative powers develop in that happy equilibrium which is the soul of beauty and the condition of humanity.*[2]

And what kind of phenomenon is it that marks the entry of the savage into humanity? If we examine history, it is the same with all peoples who have been freed from the slavery of an animal existence: the pleasure in *appearance*, and an inclination to *ornamentation* and *play*.

There is a degree of affinity between the most profound stupidity and the most profound intellect in that both seek only the *real*, and are quite unmoved by mere appearance. The first is torn from its slumber only by the immediate presentation of an object to its senses, and the second rests only when its concepts can be linked to the facts of experience. In short, stupidity cannot move beyond actuality, while intellect cannot stop short of truth. What in the former is brought about by lack of imagination is in the latter brought about by its absolute mastery. Insofar as need for reality and dependence on the actual are merely the results of a deficiency, indifference towards reality and an interest in appearance represent a real shift for mankind and a decisive step in the direction of culture. The first testifies to an external liberty, for so long as want dictates, and need compels, the power of imagination is strictly fettered to the actual; only when need is quieted does imagination develop its unhindered potential. But it also bears testimony to an inner freedom, allowing us to glimpse a power that can set itself in motion independently of external stimulus, possessing energy sufficient to ward off the matter pressing upon it. The reality of things is their own creation; the appearance of things is the work of man, and a soul that feeds on appearance no longer takes pleasure in what it receives, but instead in what it does.†

* One can read on this what Herder has written in the thirteenth book of his *Ideas Towards a Philosophy of the History of Mankind* on the proximate causes of Greek intellectual development.
† It should be perfectly clear here that this involves only aesthetic appearance, which is distinguished from reality and truth, and not logical appearance, which is, however, confused with them – and one consequently loves appearance because it is appearance, not because it is thought to be something better. Only the first is play, since the second is mere deception. Endorsing

It is nature itself that raises man from reality to appearance, arming him with two senses that lead him through appearance to the real. The eye and the ear redirect the matter pressing upon them away from the senses, depriving us of the immediacy of an object that we directly touch in our animal senses. What we *see* through the eye is different from what we *feel*; for intellect leaps straight from light and shape to things. That which we touch is a force to which we are subject; that which we see and hear with eye and ear is a form that we create. So long as man remains a savage he is diverted only through his sense of touch, which during this time serves only the sense of appearance. He either does not see, or his satisfaction does not come from this. Once he finds enjoyment in his eye, and seeing becomes something to value for itself, then he is already liberated aesthetically, and the playful impulse has begun.

And as the playful impulse stirs, taking pleasure in appearance, so it is followed by the formative impulse of imitation which treats appearance as something autonomous. Once man has become able to distinguish appearance from reality, form from body, then he is capable of separating them, for he has already done so in distinguishing them from each other. The human capacity for imitative art is therefore also given by the capacity for form; the urge for which depends upon a different endowment that I do not need to deal with here. How early or late the impulse to aesthetic art might develop will depend entirely upon the degree of love with which man is capable of remaining with simple appearance.

Since all actual existence derives from nature as an alien power, while all appearance originates with man as a thinking and imagining subject, man is only making use of his absolute right of property if he recovers appearance from essence and

appearance of the first kind cannot harm truth, since one is never in danger of taking appearance for truth, which is in fact the only thing that can be harmful to truth; to despise appearance means to despise all fine art, for it is in its essence appearance. The enthusiasm of intellect for reality can sometimes lead to such a degree of intolerance that the whole art of beautiful appearance is dismissed out of hand, just because it is appearance; but this happens to the intellect only if it recalls the affinity mentioned above. I will come back to the necessary limits of beautiful appearance on another occasion.

uses it in his own manner. As soon as he can think of linking one thing to another he is at perfect liberty to join together what nature had separated, and separate what nature had connected just as soon as he is able to separate them in his mind. Nothing is sacred here apart from his own law, once he takes note of what marks *his own* domain from the existence of things, or the realm of nature.

He exercises this human right of dominion in the *art of appearance*, and the more strictly he here separates mine and thine from each other, the more carefully he separates form from substance, and the more independence he is able to lend this form, the more will he not only extend the domain of beauty, but also maintain the boundaries of truth; because he cannot cleanse appearance of actuality without at the same time freeing actuality from appearance.

But he possesses this sovereign right only in the *realm of appearance*, in that nebulous domain of the power of imagination; and he possesses this right only so long as he conscientiously refrains from stating its existence theoretically, and refrains from lending it existence in practice. It can be seen from this that the poet likewise exceeds his bounds if he imputes existence to his ideal, and in so doing lends purpose to a particular existence. For he can only bring both about either by exceeding his right as a poet, using the ideal to encroach upon the realm of experience, seeking to render mere possibility actual existence, or by surrendering his right as a poet, allowing experience to encroach upon the realm of the ideal and restricting possibility to the conditions of the actual.

Only insofar as appearance is *sincere* (expressly abjuring all claim to reality), and only insofar as it is *autonomous* (renouncing all support from reality), is appearance aesthetic. As soon as it is false and simulates reality, as soon as it is impure and has need of reality for its effect, then it is no more than a petty tool for material ends, and provides no evidence of any freedom of spirit. It is incidentally not at all necessary that the thing in which we discover beautiful appearance is without reality, if only our judgement of this thing takes no account of this reality; for, insofar as it is taken into account, it is not an aesthetic judgement. A living female beauty will certainly please us just as much as an equally beautiful painted portrait, even a little more; but insofar as the former is more pleasing than the latter (and here I set no limits to art), this greater pleasure is not the result of autonomous appearance, is not more pleasing to pure aesthetic feeling, for this responds to the living only as appearance, and the real only as idea; and it certainly requires an incomparably higher level of fine culture to sense only pure appearance in the living, rather than forgoing the living in appearance.

One may assume spirit and taste, together with all related excellence, in any individual or an entire people where we find this sincere and autonomous appearance – there we will see actual life governed by the ideal, honour triumphing over possession, thought over pleasure, the dream of immortality over existence. There, public opinion will be the only thing to be feared, and an olive wreath valued more highly than a purple cloak.[3] Only impotence and perversity will resort to false and needy appearance, individual men as well as entire peoples who either 'supplement reality with appearance or (aesthetic) appearance with reality' – the two are often linked – demonstrating thereby their lack of moral value and their aesthetic incapacity.*

There is nothing more commonplace than hearing certain trivial critics of the present age complain that all things solid have vanished from the world, and that being is neglected in favour of seeming. Although I in no way feel called upon to

---

* The answer to the question 'To what extent may appearance exist in the moral world?' is simply this: *to the extent that it is aesthetic appearance*, i.e. appearance that neither seeks to represent reality, nor needs to be represented by it. Aesthetic appearance can never endanger the truth of morals; where one finds otherwise, it will be demonstrated without any difficulty that the appearance was not aesthetic. Only someone who is a stranger to polite society will, for example, accept assurances of generally accepted courtesy as a sign of personal regard, and if he is deceived complain of dissimulation. A complete novice in polite society may, to be polite, seek assistance from falsity, and flatter so that he might be liked. The first lacks the sense for autonomous appearance, and so can lend it meaning only through truth; the second lacks reality, and he would gladly replace it with appearance.

defend the age from this accusation, it is plain from the broad and sweeping utterances of these strict arbiters of morality that they complain not only of false appearance, but also of sincere appearance; and that even the exceptions that they make, for example in favour of beauty, are inclined more to needy than to autonomous appearance. They not only attack the deceitful cosmetics that conceal the truth, that seek to present themselves as reality, but also work themselves up over benevolent appearance that fills emptiness, and hides poverty; even against ideal appearance that ennobles vulgarity. The hypocrisy of morals offends their strong sense of truth; it is only a shame that they include courtesy among such hypocrisy. They find fault with the fact that external glitter so often obscures true merit, but they are no less irked by the way that appearance is also required of real merit, and that inner substance should be given a pleasing form. They miss the sincerity, solidity and uprightness of earlier times, but they also want to bring back its coarse and clumsy manners, all the older awkward forms, and its former Gothic exuberance. Through judgements of this kind they demonstrate a regard *for substance in itself* that is unworthy of mankind; whereas such material should be valued according to the shape it can be given, and is capable of extending the realm of ideas. Contemporary taste need pay little attention to such voices so long as it can stand its ground before a higher example. It is not that we place value upon aesthetic appearance (we have not done this nearly enough);[4] but rather that we have not yet attained the level of pure appearance, that we have not yet sufficiently distinguished existence from appearance, and in so doing secured both boundaries once and for all time – this is what a strict judge of beauty can accuse us of. And we shall deserve this accusation for so long as we are unable to enjoy the beauty of living nature without desiring it, and admire the beauty of imitative art without asking after any purpose – not admitting to the power of imagination any absolute right of its indicating instead its worth by the regard that we show for its works.

TWENTY-SEVENTH LETTER

You need have no fear for reality and truth if the elevated concept of aesthetic appearance put forward in the previous letters were to become general. For it will not become so while man is uncultivated enough to abuse it; and if it did become general, this could only be brought about by a culture that made any such abuse impossible. The pursuit of autonomous appearance calls for a greater capacity for abstraction, greater freedom of the heart, more energy of the will than man needs to limit himself to reality; and he must have already left this behind if he does wish to take up such a pursuit. What a poor choice he would make if he chose the path to the ideal so that he might spare himself the trouble of taking the path to actuality and truth! We would not need to worry very much about actuality when it came to appearance, as here understood; nonetheless, one might have greater concern about the effect of actuality upon appearance. Chained to the material world, man is long content to pursue his own ends before he allows appearance its own personality in the art of the ideal. This last calls for a total revolution in his entire way of feeling, without which he would never find himself *on the way* to the ideal. Wherever we encounter traces of a disinterested and free evaluation of pure appearance we can conclude that this kind of revolution in his nature has taken place, and infer the real beginning of humanity in him. But we do already find traces of this kind even in the first crude efforts he makes to *beautify* his existence, efforts which are made despite the risk that he might thereby worsen it with respect to its sensuous content. Once he begins to favour form over material, and risk reality for the sake of appearance (which he must recognize as such), he escapes his animal existence and finds himself on a path that never ends.

Being unsatisfied with what is sufficient for nature and what need demands, he demands much more: to begin with, certainly, just more *material* so as to conceal from appetite its limits, to secure enjoyment beyond that of immediate need; but soon a *surplus* in material, an aesthetic surplus to meet the needs of the formal impulse, to extend enjoyment beyond any need. By simply accumulating stocks for future use he anticipates the pleasure in their consumption, going beyond the present moment without, however, transcending time: he enjoys *more*, but does not change *what* he enjoys. However, since he now also includes outer form in his enjoyment, taking note of the form of the things that satisfy his appetites, he goes beyond time itself, having not merely enhanced his enjoyment in extent and degree, but also ennobled the way in which he gains such enjoyment.

Of course, nature has provided more than is immediately necessary even to those without reason, spreading a glimmer of freedom in that dark animal existence. If the lion is not gnawed by hunger, and not challenged by struggle with other predators, his idle strength becomes something in itself; the echoing desert is filled with his defiant roar, and his luxuriant strength is displayed for no purpose. Insects swarm full of life in the sunlight; and it is certainly no expression of appetite that we hear in the melodious tones of the songbird. There can be no doubt that there is freedom in all of this; not freedom from need as such, but only from a particular external need. The animal *works* when want provides the spur to its activity; and it *plays* when the spur is sheer surplus energy, when overflowing life is itself the spur to activity. Even inanimate nature displays the same luxuriance of energy and a laxity in purpose that one could in that material sense call play. The tree produces countless buds that rot without opening, and more roots, branches and leaves reach out for nourishment than are needed for the maintenance of itself and its species. What it gives back to the elements from its wasteful profusion, unused and unenjoyed, is a feast entirely at the carefree disposal of life in joyful motion. In this way nature provides us with a preliminary glimpse into the unlimited, and here *in part* removes those shackles that it does entirely without in the realm of form. This movement from the compulsion of need, or *physical gravity*, to the compulsion of surplus, or *physical play*, represents the transition to aesthetic play; and before nature moves up into the higher liberty of the beautiful, beyond the shackles of any purpose, it verges upon this autonomy at least in its *free movement*, which is itself both means and end.

Like the body's organs, man's power of imagination also has its free movement and material play, enjoying its own absolute and untrammelled power without any relationship to shape or form. To the degree that nothing of form plays a part in this play of imagination, the whole charm of which consists in an unforced association of images, such play belongs merely to man's animal life even though such imagination is proper to man alone; it is proof of his liberation from any external sensuous compulsion, without it yet being possible to conclude that man possesses an autonomous formative power.*
From this play of *freely associated ideas*, which is still quite material in nature and to be explained by simple natural laws, the power of imagination finally makes the leap to aesthetic play in attempting to find *a free form*. It has to be called a leap, because here a completely new power comes into play; for the first time a deliberating spirit mixes itself with the actions of blind instinct, subordinating the arbitrary processes

* Most of the imaginative play that occurs in everyday life rests either entirely upon these feelings for the free association of ideas, or borrows its greatest charm from the same. However little this proves in itself for a higher nature, and however gladly even the slackest souls might be inclined to surrender themselves to this free flow of images, this independence of imagination from external impressions is in fact the negative condition of its creative capacity. Only by detaching itself from actuality does forming power raise itself into an ideal, and before imagination in its productive qualities can operate according to its own laws it must have first, in its reproductive processes, already freed itself from alien laws. It is, of course, a big step from mere lawlessness to autonomously creating one's own laws, and this also requires a completely new power – the capacity for ideas – but this power can then the more easily develop because the senses no longer work against it, and the indefinite borders upon the infinite, at least negatively.

of the power of imagination to its unchanging eternal unity, places its own autonomy in the transitory and its infinity in the sensuous. But so long as raw nature remains so powerful, knowing no law other than to hurry restlessly from change to change, it will resist with its inconstant arbitrariness that necessity, opposing constancy with unrest, autonomy with neediness, and sublime simplicity with discontent. Hence in its preliminary endeavours the aesthetic playful impulse will be barely recognizable, being continually interrupted by the sensuous impulse with its wilful moodiness and wild appetites, confusing the supreme necessity of the ideal with the meagre condition of the individual, and soiling the noble presentation of an eternal will, in fine form, with the impure trace of transitory desire. Thus we see crude taste seizing upon the new and surprising, what is colourful, adventurous and bizarre, the violent and the savage – and shunning above all simplicity and tranquillity. It fashions grotesque shapes, favours sudden, abrupt changes, opulent forms, clashing contrasts, garish colours, emotional song. During this era he considers beautiful merely that which stimulates him, what gives him material – but excites in him an automatic resistance; but it is material that first provides the prospect of *working and shaping*, for otherwise it would not be beauty, even for him. And so in the form of his judgements a remarkable change takes place: he seeks these things not because they render him passive, but because they make him active; they do not please him because they satisfy a need, but because they correspond to a law which speaks to him in his own breast, if as yet only quietly.

Soon he is no longer satisfied that things merely please him; he wants to be pleasing himself, although to begin with only with that which is *his*, ultimately with that which *he* is. What he possesses, what he makes, must no longer just bear the marks of servility, the querulous form of its function; besides the service that it represents it has to reflect the inspiration that conceived it, the loving hand that made it, the serene and free spirit that chose it and placed it on display. Now the ancient German seeks glossier pelts, more imposing antlers, more intricate drinking horns, and the Caledonian chooses the nicest mussels for his feast.[1] Even weapons must no longer be simple objects of terror, but also be pleasing to the eye, and the highly decorated sword belt will be no less remarked upon than the deadly blade of the sword. Not content with bringing an aesthetic surplus into the necessary, the free impulse to play finally tears itself free of the bonds of bare necessity, and the beautiful becomes in itself an object for his efforts. He *adorns* himself. Simple pleasure becomes one of his needs, and soon the best part of his pleasures derives from what is unnecessary.

Just as form slowly approaches from without, in his home, his household goods and his clothing, so it finally begins to take possession of him, transforming first the external man, and then the inner. Random leaps of joy turn into dance, the unformed movement of a limb becomes part of a graceful, harmonious language of gesture, the confused noises develop, begin to obey rhythm and assume the shape of song. When the Trojan army storms on to the battlefield with piercing shrieks for all the world like a flock of cranes, the Greeks approach them silently and with measured pace. In the former we see only the exuberance of blind forces; in the latter the triumph of form, and the simple majesty of the law.[2]

A finer necessity now chains the sexes together, and the heart sustains an alliance that desire can make only provisionally, according to shifting mood. Released from its grim fetters, a calmer eye can now apprehend the figure before it, one soul looks into another, and an egoistic exchange of lust becomes a generous exchange of affection. Desire grows and elevates itself into love while mankind becomes absorbed by its object, and the petty advantage over sense is spurned in favour of winning a more noble victory over the will. The need to please subordinates the powerful to the gentle judgement of taste; while he can steal lust, love must be a gift. He can fight for this higher prize only through form, not through matter. He has to cease to handle feeling as a power, and face up to intellect as appearance; he must admit freedom, because he wishes to be pleasing to it. Just as beauty resolves the conflict of natures through its most simple and pure example, in the eternal antagonism of the sexes, so it also resolves this antagonism – or at least aims to resolve it – in the most complex whole of society, reconciling everything soft and powerful in the moral world according to the framework of a free alliance of male power and female benevolence. Now the weak becomes divine, and unbridled strength dishonoured; the injustice of nature is ameliorated through the generosity of chivalric morals. He whom no violence can frighten is disarmed by the tender blush of modesty, and tears stifle a revenge that no blood could dissolve. Even hatred attends to the gentle voice of honour, the sword of the victor spares the disarmed foe, and a welcoming hearth smokes for the stranger on that dreaded shore where he would once have been met only with murder.

In the midst of the awful realm of force, and in the midst of the divine realm of law, the aesthetic impulse to form constructs unnoticed a third happy realm of play and of appearance in which the fetters of all circumstance are taken from man, releasing him from everything that could be called either moral or physical constraint.

If in the *dynamic* state of rights one man encounters another as force, and limits his impact,[3] and if he encounters another in the *ethical* state[4] of obligation and opposes him with the majesty of the law and curbs his desire, then where conduct is governed by beauty, in the *aesthetic* state,[5] he may appear to the other only as a figure, only as the object of free play. The basic law of this realm is *to give freedom by means of freedom*. Here, the individual may not dispute with the whole, nor the whole with the individual. One may not become strong through the submission of the other; here there may only be victors, and no vanquished.

The dynamic state can make society possible only by taming nature with nature; the ethical state can make it (morally) necessary only by subjecting the individual will to the general will; only the aesthetic state can make it real because it fulfils the will of the whole through the nature of the individual. If man is driven into society by his needs, and reason implants social principles within him, it is only beauty than can give him a *social character*. Taste alone introduces harmony into society, because it fosters harmony in the individual.[6] All other forms of imagination separate men, since they base themselves exclusively on either the sensuous or the spiritual side of their being; only the fine idea makes of this a whole, because his two natures must be harmonized together. All other forms of communication separate society, since they relate exclusively either to the private sensitivity or the private capacity of individual members, hence to what distinguishes man from man; only aesthetic communication unites society, because it is based upon what is shared in common. We enjoy the pleasures of the senses only as individuals without the genus living within us being part of this; we cannot make sensuous pleasures general, since we cannot generalize our own individuality. We enjoy the pleasures of knowledge only as genus, and by carefully removing all trace of individuality from our judgement; so we cannot generalize the pleasures of reason because we cannot exclude the traces of individuality from the judgements of others in the same way that we can for our own. It is only beauty that we enjoy both as individual and genus, as *representatives* of the genus. The sensuous good can render only one person happy because it is founded upon appropriation, something that always implies exclusion; this one person can also only be made happy partially, since personality here plays no part. The absolute good can make someone happy only under conditions that cannot be presumed to exist universally; for truth is the prize of denial, and only a pure heart believes in pure will. Beauty alone makes the whole world happy, and every being forgets its limits so long as it is under its spell.

No privilege, no autocracy will be tolerated as far as taste prevails and the realm of beautiful appearance holds sway. This realm reaches up into the spheres where reason rules with unconditional necessity and all matter ceases; and it reaches downwards, as far down as the natural impulse rules with blind compulsion, and form has not yet begun; but even at the most extreme frontiers, where taste is deprived of legislative power, it still does not allow its effective power to be taken from it. Unsociable desire has to surrender its self-obsession, and the agreeable, which otherwise seduces the senses, must also cast the net of grace over mind. Duty, the strong voice of necessity, has to change a censorious tone justified only by the resistance it encounters, and honour a willing nature by placing trust in a more refined one. The taste for knowledge leads out from the mysteries of science beneath the open sky of common sense, and transforms the property of the schoolroom into the common property of mankind. In its domain even the most powerful genius must acknowledge its supremacy, and trustfully assume the mind of a child. Strength must allow itself to be bound by the Graces, and the defiant lion submit to Cupid's bridle. Taste will in return throw its forgiving veil over that physical need whose nakedness offends the dignity of free spirits, concealing from us our dishonourable kinship with matter by a lovely illusion of liberty. Lent wing in this way, even the servile art paid by the piece shakes off its dust and the fetters of bondage fall from the lifeless and the living alike, touched by taste's wand. In the aesthetic state everyone is a free citizen, even those who are no more than tools: free citizens who have rights equal to the most noble, and intellect which violently bends the acquiescent mass to its ends has here to seek assent. Thus the ideal of equality is fulfilled here in the realm of aesthetic appearance, an ideal that the enthusiast would so keenly like to see realized in its essence; and if it is true that fine breeding matures most quickly and completely in the vicinity of the throne, one would also have to recognize here the benevolent dispensation that seems often only to limit man in the real world, the better to launch him into an ideal one.[*7]

---

* Does such a state of aesthetic appearance exist, and where can it be found? As a need, it exists in every finely tuned soul; as a fact, one could find it only in a few selected circles, like the pure Church and the pure republic, where conduct is guided not by the mindless imitation of foreign morals, but by our own fine nature; where man proceeds through the most involved circumstances with alert simplicity and tranquil innocence, and finds no need of offending alien liberty in order to claim one's own, nor of discarding one's own dignity in order to manifest grace. Since no good state should lack a constitution, such a constitution can be demanded of the aesthetic state. I know of none of this kind, and so I might hope that my first sketch of the same, which I have determined for this journal, will be received with appreciation.

LETTERS TO PRINCE FREDERICK CHRISTIAN VON AUGUSTENBURG

Most serene Prince,

That I have remained silent for so long is an affront to myself, and not to you; for which I more deserve your pity than your displeasure.

Throughout this time I have been a victim of hypochondria, very uncertain of my health, as if my physical and mental powers were crippled; I felt myself quite incapable of arousing that cheerful state of mind I would so much like to show you. But in the few sunny moments in my life so far I have at least sought to be not entirely without value to you, my eternally venerated Prince; I was, throughout the entire time, constantly concerned and occupied with providing you, together with your noble friends, with a sample of my efforts. My hope was quite definitely that I would complete the work this winter, then being able to deliver into those hands what truly belonged to them; for who else but your most excellent self do I have to thank for the long-desired and inestimable good fortune of being able to pursue freely my own inclination? However, circumstance dictated so many interruptions that I can now only hope to complete this work by the end of the summer, and even then with some difficulty. Nonetheless, since my health seems to be slowly recovering, I feel better able to look to the future in good spirits.

The venture upon which I embarked, most gracious Prince – for now that I am in confessional mood I wish to conceal nothing – is I admit somewhat daring, but an irresistible inclination drew me to it. My present inability to practise the skill

proper to an open and free mind favoured me with the need
to reflect upon its principles. The revolution that has occurred
in the world of philosophy has rocked the foundations upon
which aesthetics was built, and its former system, if one can
call it such, has been toppled. I do not need to tell you, my
Prince, that in his critique of aesthetic judgement Kant has
already begun to apply the principles of critical philosophy to
questions of taste; preparing, if not providing, the foundations
for a new theory of art.[1] Nevertheless, with the philosophical
world as it now is, attention will ultimately turn to aesthetics,
and it will be regenerated. Our best thinkers still have their
hands full with metaphysics, and now natural law and politics seem to call for closer attention. Little light appears to
reach the philosophy of art from this direction; and at a time
when the human mind is illuminating and reordering all areas
of knowledge, it alone could well remain in the obscurity with
which we are familiar.

I believe that it deserves a better fate, and have determined
upon the bold idea of becoming its knight. For the time being I
just have a few passing ideas, since my vocation as a philosopher is as yet undecided; but I will seek to pursue it. For
the foundation of a theory of art it is not enough, I think, to
be a philosopher; one has to have practised the art oneself,
and this, I believe, lends me some advantage over those who
will without doubt be superior to me in philosophical insight.
Somewhat lengthy practice in art has allowed me to observe
nature's workings in me in ways that cannot be learned from
books. More than any of my other colleagues in Germany, I
have learned through *mistakes*; and this, I believe, leads to a
clearer insight into the sanctuary of art than the insight gained
by the certain course of unerring genius. This is what I can say
in advance by way of justifying my enterprise; success alone
will judge the rest.

And with you, my venerable Prince, I will need no apology
when seeking to raise the most efficient of all springs of the
human spirit, the soul-forming fine arts, to the rank of a philosophical science. When I reflect upon the connection that joins
the sense of the beautiful and the great to the most noble part

of our being, I simply cannot consider this connection to be a merely subjective play of the power of sensation, capable of no more than empirical laws. As with truth and justice, beauty must also, I think, rest on eternal foundations, and the original laws of reason must also be laws of taste. Of course, the circumstance that we *sense* beauty and do not recognize it seems to nullify all hope that we might find a generally valid principle for it, for here every judgement is merely a judgement from experience. Usually one considers an explanation of beauty to be confirmed because it is in each individual instance in agreement with the expression of feeling; for if there really were a knowledge of the beautiful based upon principles, one could trust the expression of feeling only because it was in agreement with the explanation of the beautiful. Instead of testing and correcting one's feelings according to principles, aesthetic principles are tested against one's feelings.

This is the knot that unfortunately even Kant thought indissoluble. What, most dear Prince, will you say to the idea of a beginner who has only momentarily glanced into the temple of philosophy, but who nonetheless pursues a solution to this problem in the face of a declaration by such a man? In fact, I would never have had sufficient courage if Kant's philosophy had not itself given me the means. This fruitful philosophy, of which it is so often said that it only ever tears down, and never builds up, in my opinion provides the solid foundation stone upon which a system of aesthetics can be constructed; and I perceive this only by virtue of an earlier idea of Kant's that was not recognized as such. I lay no claim to be the only one to have understood this; I seek only to establish how far this discovered path will lead me. Even if it leads nowhere, no journey is entirely wasted when searching for the truth.

This leads me to a request, most admirable Prince, which I hope you might grant. I wished that my ideas on the philosophy of the beautiful be developed in a series of individual letters addressed to you, and which I could then lay before the public. This freer form would lend their presentation more individuality and life; and the idea that I addressed you, and was judged by you, would give me a greater interest in my material. Few mortals combine a pure and lucid sense of truth with a warm receptiveness for everything beautiful and good and great, and the majority of our scholars are so fearfully buckled into their systems that a somewhat unfamiliar form of presentation cannot penetrate their triply armoured chests. There are few whose tender feelings for beauty are not smothered by abstraction, and even fewer think it worth the trouble to philosophize on their feelings. I must entirely forget that I will be judged by such people; I can develop my ideas and feelings only for free and open minds which range beyond the dust of schools, and which retain within themselves the sparks of pure and noble humanity.

Please, then, allow me, my eternally and highly esteemed Prince, to make such a rare gift, assuring me of your graciousness, seeking to master the noble bond that is woven by philosophy and taste between the friends of wisdom and beauty, disregarding all social distance in our relationship. These two deities will for me mark the boundaries within which I might make use of this freedom, and which will never permit me to extend my wishes further than those few moments from a life devoted to the happiness of the world that you might give to my philosophical and poetical visions.

With the greatest respect and love etc.

Saturday, 13 July 1793, Jena

Most serene Prince,

How very much you have honoured me by the gracious acceptance of my request that I might present to you the results of my investigations of the beautiful in a series of letters. If my pleasure in this inestimable proof of your benevolence could have been increased in any way, it would have been in the explanation that accompanied the permission that you gave. You decreed, dearest Prince, that I be bound by fetters of a dogmatic lecture, and obliged me to do what I *had* asked as a favour. The freedom of the presentation that Your Serenity requests is not for me a constraint, but a need; you generously leave me the appearance of a service where I have in fact no choice. I am too little acquainted with academic formalities to err by abusing them; I will therefore at least be certain of *the* danger of *methodically* tiring your patience. My philosophy will not deny its origin; and if you come to grief, it will be more in the depths and eddies of the power of poetic imagination than on the barren sands of dry abstraction. If you find fault with the fruit of my own reflection, formed from my own limited experience, it will not be on account of its sectarian nature; it will fail because of its own fragility, and not seek to uphold itself by appeal to authority and external assistance. Even where I link my argument to Critical Philosophy (and I do not deny that this might happen very often), I hope to respect the liberty of your mind and gain the voluntary assent of your independent reason.

Some Kantian statements are lent a rigour and singularity alien to their substance by the strict purity and scholastic form with which they are phrased; and if stripped of this mantle, they are then revealed as the expired claims of common reason. I have often remarked that philosophical truths have to be found in another form, and applied and diffused in yet another. The beauty of a building is not apparent until the apparatus of stonemason and carpenter is removed, and the scaffolding behind which it rose is broken up. But the majority of Kant's students have allowed themselves to be carried away more by the spirit of his system than by its machinery, thereby making plain that they are more labourer than master builder.

I cannot tell you enough, most excellent Prince, how pleasantly surprised I was by your admission that you had been poorly served by the intolerance of our philosophical utopians; that you also extend this concern to me increases, if that is possible, my deep respect for your mind, and heightens my trust, for this is the sole flaw from which I hope to remain free. Your liberal way of thought creates for me the fortunate liberty of simply following my own conviction, independent of any system. The realm of reason is a realm of freedom; no servitude is more shameful than that which is tolerated on this holy ground. Many who settle there, but lack the inner capacity, prove they were not born free, but only set free.

If I should, however, confirm your fears, merciful Prince, despite my active dislike of a love of system, and lose myself in the infertile steppes of speculation, you will send the Graces to my assistance, calling the wanderer back to the proper path. I beg you to give me nothing, and forgive me for nothing. Do not allow me to fight the cause of beauty with weapons unworthy of beauty, offending the rules of taste in the very moment that I seek to prove their validity.

But should I perhaps not be able to make better use of the freedom that Your Serenity allows me than by presenting to you my ideas of beauty and fine art? Is it *not at all the time* to be so concerned with the needs of the *aesthetic* world, when the affairs of the *political* world present a much more immediate interest?

I love art and everything related to it above all else, and I admit that my inclination is to favour it before any other occupation of the mind. But it is not here a matter of what art is *to me*, but rather how it relates to the human spirit as a whole; in particular, how it relates to the *time* at which I present myself as its advocate.

I would not willingly live in another century, and influence another. One is just as much a citizen of the era as one is a citizen of the world, or of a state, or head of a household. If it is thought improper and impermissible to detach oneself from the customs and usages of the people among whom one lives, and the circle in which one is at home, why should it be any less a duty to orient the choice of one's activity according to the tastes and needs of the era?

One could say perhaps that what is good in itself, is good for all time, and that is so for every inquiry into the truth. But there are many truths to study, and in choosing among them I think that the needs and tastes of the time deserve a priority.

However, this priority does not seem to favour the fine arts at all. The course of events in political life and that of the human spirit in literary life have lent the genius of the age a direction that increasingly distances it from *idealizing* art. This has to detach itself from actuality and, with some audacity, raise itself above the needs of the present, for art is the daughter of freedom. But now need prevails, the force of the physical situation, the dependency of man upon a thousand relationships that bind him, increasingly binding him into an un-ideal actuality, hindering free flight into the regions of the ideal. Even speculative reason robs one province after another of the power of imagination, and the boundaries of art become more limited, the more that *science* extends its own.

At present it is the work of political creation that preoccupies practically every mind. The events of this final decade of the eighteenth century are no less a challenge and important for philosophers than they are for the active *man of the world*, and Your Serenity could thus have two reasons to expect that I make this remarkable material the object of the written communication that you have allowed me with such generosity and benevolence.

A law of the wise Solon condemned the citizen who failed to choose a side in an insurrection.[2] If there were ever a case to which this law might be applied then it would be the present, in which the great fate of mankind is brought into question, and in which it seems that no one can remain neutral without being guilty of the most culpable indifference to what must be most holy to man. A spirited and courageous nation, long regarded as a model, has begun to depart violently from its actual civil condition and return to that natural state for which Reason is the sole and absolute legislator. However much the *substance* and *consequences* of this great legal business might be of interest to anyone who calls himself a man, the *manner in which it is conducted* must make it of especial interest to anyone who can think for himself. Something which has hitherto been decided by the right of the strongest and convenience has now been made dependent upon the judgement of *pure reason*, and pretends at least that it wishes to be judged according to *principles*. However, every man who can think for himself (insofar as he is capable of generalizing his particular way of thinking, extending his individuality to the human race) can consider himself as a participant in this Court of Reason, woven into the outcome of proceedings both as man and as citizen of the world. Not only does this legal process involve *him*, but its decision is made according to *laws* that he is, as participating representative of Reason, entitled to dictate, and which he is obliged to uphold.

What could, excellent Prince, be more attractive and interesting for me than to delve into this great matter together with such an inspired thinker and humane citizen of the world who embraces all of humanity with such great enthusiasm, whose lucid and unprejudiced sense of reason radiates pure and undistorted? A conversation about such matters would have all the greater attraction for me the more that the position from which *I*, a private person, regard the political world differs from that from which *you*, a prince and ruling statesman, look down into the flow of events. What could be more delightful than to meet each other in the *way of thinking* just where external *relationships* bring about the greatest distance, converging on the same midpoint in the world of ideas from such an immeasurable distance in the actual world?

That I resist this attractive temptation, and bring to the written conversation that Your Serenity allows me material that is so removed from the talk of the epoch, is not from any overwhelming inclination for this object, even though I would never be ashamed of such an inclination; it is not my preference for art, but a principle that is determined by choice; and I believe that I can justify it. If I can in the *treatment* of my object lay claim to your indulgence, then I would gladly earn your approval for such a choice.

If the fact were true – if the extraordinary case occurred that political legislation were put in the charge of Reason, man was respected and treated as an independent being, law was elevated to the throne, and true freedom made into the foundation of the state edifice – then I would wish to take my eternal leave of the Muses, so that I might devote all my activity to the most wonderful of all creations, the monarchy of Reason. But this is the very fact that I dare to doubt. Indeed, I am so far removed from belief in any regeneration of political life that, instead, the events of our time rob me of all hope for centuries.

Before these events occurred, merciful Prince, it was possible to flatter oneself with the comfortable illusion that the unnoticed but unbroken influence of thinkers, the germs of wisdom scattered through the centuries, and the accumulated treasure of experience would gradually render souls more receptive to the better, and so prepare for an epoch in which philosophy took over the moral construction of the world, and light could triumph over darkness. One had advanced so far with theoretical culture that the most sacred pillars of superstition were rocked, and the throne of thousand-year-old prejudice began to shake. Nothing was wanting save the *signal* for the great transformation, and a union of souls. Both of these have now happened – but what is the outcome?

The attempt by the French people to realize themselves in their sacred rights of man and thereby achieve political freedom has merely revealed their own incapacity and unworthiness, casting not only this unhappy people, but also, with them, a considerable part of Europe, back a whole century in barbarism and servitude. The moment was the most favourable, but it found a corrupted generation unworthy of it, which knew neither how to appreciate it, nor how to make use of it. The use that it makes and has made of this great gift of chance proves indisputably that the human race has not yet grown out of the force of tutelage, that the liberal regime of Reason there comes too soon, where one will be scarcely capable of resisting the brutal force of animality, and that the time is not yet ripe for *civil* liberty, since so much that is *human* is absent.

Man defines himself by his deeds – and what kind of image of man do we see in the mirror of our present times? Here the most disgusting degeneration, there the most contrasting extreme of enervation; the two most sorry aberrations into which the human character can sink, united within one epoch.

In the lower classes we see nothing but crude, lawless impulses set free by the abolition of the constraint of civil order, hastening with ungovernable fury to satiate their animal wants. It was not their inner moral resistance that hitherto contained their irruption, but only external compulsion. And so they were not free men whom the state had oppressed; no, they were merely wild animals that the state had bound with benevolent chains. If the state had really oppressed mankind, as it is accused of doing, then humanity would stand revealed once the state was destroyed. But the removal of *external* oppression merely renders *inner* oppression visible, and the wild despotism of impulse releases all those misdeeds that make us both nauseous and fearful.

On the other hand, the civilized classes present to us the even more repugnant sight of enervation, of moral degeneration, a decline of character that is all the more disgusting the more that culture plays a part in it. I no longer recall which of the ancient or modern philosophers made the remark that the depravity of those who were more noble was the more repulsive, but experience confirms that in this case. Once culture begins to degenerate it descends into a far more vile corruption than barbarism ever experiences. The sensuous man cannot fall lower than the animal; but if the enlightened man degenerates he goes to the devil, and plays nefariously with that which is most holy for humanity.

The Enlightenment, which the higher ranks of our age are not wrong in extolling, is merely theoretical culture, and on the whole shows so little refining influence on sensibility that it rather more helps make a system out of corruption, rendering it incurable. A refined and consistent Epicureanism has begun to smother all energy of character, and the ever more tightly binding fetters of need, the progressive dependence of mankind upon the physical, have brought us to a condition in which the maxims of passivity and passive obedience count as the supreme rules of life, hence of limitation in thought, powerlessness in action, dreadful mediocrity in creativity, all of which are characteristic of our age, to its great disgrace. And so we see the spirit of the age caught between barbarism and enervation, freethinking and superstition, crudity and delicacy, and it is only the *equilibrium of vices* that holds everything together.

And I would like to ask: is this the mankind for whose rights the philosopher employs his time, having in mind the noble citizen of the world, and for whom a new Solon would wish to construct a new constitution? I doubt it very much. Man's claim to liberty rests only on his ability to act as a moral being; a soul capable only of sensuous stimulation is neither worthy of liberty, nor sensible of it. All lasting reforms must proceed from a way of thought; where principles are corrupted nothing healthy, nothing good can blossom. The state is created and maintained through the character of its citizens, making political and civic liberty possible. For if wisdom personified were to descend from Olympus to introduce the most perfect constitution, it would still be man who had to make it work.

If, gracious Prince, I might be permitted to express my opinion about contemporary political needs and expectations, then I admit that I consider any attempt to create a state constitution upon principles – anything else being merely provisional patchwork – to be untimely; that all hopes for this are mere enthusiasm so long as the character of mankind has not been raised from the depths of its decay; which is itself the work of more than a century. One might well hear from time to time of an abuse that has been ended, of the success of some fortunate reform, of some triumph of reason over prejudice;

but whatever ten great men build will just as surely be torn down again by fifty dolts. In other parts of the world the negro will be set free from his chains, while in Europe minds will be enchained. So long as the supreme principle of states is stamped with a shocking selfishness, and so long as the citizen cares only for his physical well-being, then so long, I fear, will the political regeneration which was believed to be so imminent remain a nice philosophical dream.

Should one therefore cease to strive for this? Should the most important of all human affairs be left at the mercy of legal caprice, to blind chance, while all other aspects of the domain of reason are extended? Nothing less, gracious Prince. Political and civic freedom remains eternally the most sacred of all things, the most deserving aim of all effort, the great centre of all culture; but this wondrous structure can only be built on the solid foundation of an ennobled character. One has to begin with the creation of the citizens for a constitution, before these citizens can be granted a constitution.

Perhaps you may object, most serene Prince, that we have a circular argument here: that the character of a citizen depends just as much upon a constitution as that constitution depends on the citizen's character. I admit that, and so claim that, if we wish to break out of this circularity, we must *either* think of means of assisting the state without involving character, *or* deal with character without involving the state. The first contains a contradiction, for no constitution can be conceived that is independent of the disposition of the citizen. However, perhaps there is something in the second idea, so that sources independent of the state might be made capable of refining ways of thought, but which sources for all their faults do uphold the state in a pure and open manner.

As is known, character is worked upon through the *correction of concepts* and the *purification of feelings*. The first is the task of *philosophical* culture, the latter that of *aesthetic* culture. The clarification of concepts is not enough, for it is a long way from head to heart, and the overwhelming majority of men are moved to act through sensations. But the heart is by itself an uncertain guide, and the most delicate sensation is all the more easily hostage to enthusiasm if not governed by good sense. Healthiness of the mind must be linked to purity of the will if character is to be considered complete.

It seems to me that the pressing need of our era is the refinement of feelings and the moral purification of the will; since plenty enough has already been done for the enlightenment of understanding. It is not so much that we lack knowledge of truth and justice, but that we do not know the effect of this knowledge on the direction of the will: not so much in respect of *light* as in respect of *warmth*, not so much in philosophical as in aesthetic culture. I regard the latter as the most effective means in the formation of character, being both completely independent of political circumstance and requiring no assistance from the state.

And it is here, gracious Prince, that art and taste lay their shaping hand upon man, demonstrating their improving influence. The arts of the beautiful and the sublime promote life, practise and refine the capacity for sensation; they raise the mind from gross material pleasures to pure appreciation of mere form, and make it accustomed to combine voluntary action in its pleasures. However, the true refinement of feelings always consists in a balance between the higher nature of man and the divine part of his being, his reason and his freedom.

> If sense's pleasure and sense's pain,
> Entangled around the heart of man,
> Entangled by a thousand knots,
> Drag him down into the dust,
> Who will protect him? Who will save him?
> The arts, which draw him
> Upwards to freedom on golden rings,
> Charmed by refinement that
> Hovers him between earth and heaven.[3]

Of course, it cannot be denied that art – both poetic and figurative – clings gladly to the spirit of the century. If *discriminating* taste turns to the base and the bad, then it is not unusual for *productive* taste to do likewise, for the artist is formed in part by the age in which he lives, and seeks its approval. But even if he is permitted to adhere to the spirit of the century, he should not take direction from it. The guiding laws of art do not take their form from a changing and often quite degenerated contemporary taste, but are founded in the necessity and eternity of human nature, in the original laws of the spirit. The pure source of beauty streams down from the divine part of our being, from the eternally pure ether of ideal mankind, uninfected by the spirit of the age that seethes in the dark eddies far below. It is for this reason that art can, in the midst of a barbaric and unworthy century, remain pure like a goddess, so long as its higher origin is remembered, and it does not itself become slave to base intentions and needs. It is in this way that the few remnants of the *Greek spirit* wander through the night of our Nordic age,[4] and the electric shock of this spirit arouses some related souls to a sense of their greatness.

If art is not to suffer the misfortune of sinking into imitation of the spirit of the age, which it should instead raise up to its level, then it has to have *ideals* which constantly keep before it an image of the supremely beautiful, whatever the degradation of the age; it must have its own *code* that can preserve it securely both from the despotism of a local and unilateral taste and from the anarchy of a feral barbarism.[5] It already possesses ideals, in part, in the immortal models handed down from the Greeks and some more recent genius, and which, eternally untouched, survive every change of fashion in taste. But it has hitherto lacked a code, and its creation is one of the most difficult problems that philosophical reason can assume – for what can be more difficult than to subsume the work of genius to principles, and to unite liberty with necessity.

Might I not flatter myself overmuch, gracious Prince, to hope to have convinced you that a philosophy of the beautiful is not so removed from the needs of the time as it might seem, and that this object is even worthy of the attention of the political philosopher, since every fundamental improvement of the state has to begin with the refinement of character, which can be effected through the beautiful and the sublime? But perhaps my preference for the sciences and fine arts has persuaded me to trust to effects of which they are not capable. Perhaps I should have made quite clear the influence of aesthetic culture upon moral culture. So permit me, most merciful Prince, to leave this proof for the following letter, since this one has already exceeded its bounds.

I trust that Your Serenity has not been put off by this, my first attempt to clothe unyielding nature in the light mantle of a letter, and that my conversation has pleased you! Now that I have begun I can follow up rather more quickly, now that I have charted the landscape through which your attention will accompany me; and that was why I took so much time to write this first letter. Now I am entirely free, and will take full measure of the gracious permission that Your Serenity has been good enough to grant me.

At the same time I take the liberty of including a printed article whose content is related, in which I announced some of these ideas and wrote them down, and whose more detailed development will now occupy me.[6]

Baggesen,[7] who is at the moment still here, lends me very pleasant hours, and the most delightful among them are always those in which he sketches for us the image of a prince who is the most inexhaustible object of his heart, and who will remain always one of the dearest, from the heart of one who calls himself with deepest devotion and awe,

    etc.

In the period that has elapsed between the sending of this and the previous letter I have returned to my fatherland after many years of exile;[8] I have become the father of a son; and withstood renewed and wearying episodes of my old illness. This conjunction of happy abandonment and sadder events delayed the completion and dispatch of this letter, and I now lose not one moment in taking up the thread of an argument that had been broken off. How encouraging was Your Serenity's assurance that this exchange of letters provided you with some diversion, and that you would not be displeased to find the exchange quickening in pace. I also hope to show you in its course that if I have hitherto fallen short of your expectations and my own wishes it is not my fault, but rather that of my fate.

But any obligation on my side cannot of course involve any on your own side, excellent Prince. Each stroke of the pen from your hand with which you answer my letter will be a precious gift for me; but I will never allow myself to expect it. There is nothing I would fear more than infringing the liberty of those whom I esteem and love. I was prompted to make this explanation by one very flattering passage in your letter, in which Your Serenity seeks to give me a reason for the delay in your reply.

Baggesen has portrayed Your Serenity in exactly the way that Graff in Dresden and any good portrait painter would.[9] He gave you no alien features, and this alone I call the flattery of portraiture; he simply idealized your own, and the sketch that he made of you for me was more highly coloured, as an expression of his feelings. Improving on a character and idealizing a character are for me two very different things. The latter can be done only by an excellent artist; the former is the usual approach of the mediocre. Each individual human character is at the same time its own species, and the momentary modes of appearance are only variations of this species. These momentary modes of appearance are partly coincidental since transitory external circumstances influence them; and because they do not depend on character alone, they cannot represent a true image of a character. To gain this true image one has to know how to separate the underlying inner and lasting aspects from the accidental; the species or the generic nature of this individuality must be found – and that is what I call idealizing a portrait. The individuality of a character not only loses nothing in such an operation, but also can be discovered only in this one way; for because the accidental and the external influence has been detached, the inner and lasting aspects will remain in an all the more pure state. Of course, an image drafted in this manner will not at any one moment fully resemble the original, but it will be a truer likeness as a whole.

Perhaps without either knowledge or intention, Baggesen has sketched such a likeness of Your Serenity for me, and the striking coincidence of this portrait with everything that your mind and heart has revealed to me assures me that his depiction is genuine. Permit me therefore, most worthy Prince, to show you the fairness that you seem to deny yourself.

In a few passages of my previous letters I have expressed myself somewhat indefinitely, and the acute observations made by Your Serenity give me the opportunity to correct this mistake. I have limited the need of our time to practical education, and given a rather more favourable account of the theoretical culture of our century than you, gracious Prince, believe it yet deserves. Perhaps I can remove your doubts by a more exact explanation.

It is entirely true, as Your Serenity claims, that the greatest part of the evil of which we complain in the current century is caused by the lack of sufficient correction given to concepts and prejudices, and testifies to a darkening of minds that does little honour to the Age of Enlightenment. The lack of theoretical culture is therefore indeed one of the most immediate causes of the degeneration that has struck our contemporaries down – one of the most immediate causes, but not the most immediate. For I ask again: where does this lack of theoretical culture come from, given the giant steps made by philosophy, given all the light provided by a more thorough knowledge of nature, a deeper knowledge of man and his relationships, plus all the efforts made by thinking men to diffuse this knowledge and make it generally available? The storehouse is full and opened up to all the world, and the most petty human intellect can find light and truth there – why are there so few who make use of it? The epoch is enlightened, by which I mean, the knowledge which could correct our concepts has actually been discovered and established. A more healthy philosophy has undermined the dubious ideas upon which superstition raised its shadowy throne – so why is this throne still standing? Our politics, our legislation, our public law has considered a better morality, and the barbaric features in our habits, the faults in our laws, and the illogicalities in our conventions and customs have been revealed – so why is it that we remain barbarians nonetheless?

There must be something in the souls of men that obstructs the acceptance of truth even when it shines so brightly, and which prevents the possession of something better, which is paraded only for show. The Ancients guessed it, and it lies hidden in the expression *sapere aude*.[10]

Dare to know. Strength and energy of decision are also part of overcoming obstacles, both of the natural idleness of the mind and of the cowardice of the heart opposing the acceptance of truth. Not for nothing is the Goddess of Wisdom presented to us in fables as a warrior, emerging in full armour from Jupiter's head. For even the first stirring of wisdom in the head is martial. Already at birth it has to fight a fierce battle with a sensibility that is too comfortable in its alien guardian, as if it strives to bring the epoch of maturity as close as possible.

The majority of men are too tired and worn down by bitter struggle with physical need to rouse themselves to a new, inner struggle with delusion and prejudice. Their entire strength is exhausted by doing what is necessary, and if they have with great effort achieved this, the need is for rest, and not renewed mental effort. Happy that they do not need to think for themselves, they gladly allow others to take control of their ideas, a blind resignation regarding alien wisdom saving them from the bitter need to examine it for themselves. If it does happen that higher needs are aroused in head and heart, they grasp with a hungry credulity the formulae that the state and the priesthood have kept back for this moment, formulae that have always enabled them to deal with feelings of liberty aroused in their wards.

And so one will always find that the most oppressed people are the most stupid; hence the work of enlightenment in a nation has to begin by improving its physical condition. First of all, the mind must be released from the yoke of necessity before it can be led to freedom and reason. Only in this sense is it true that care for the citizen's physical well-being should be treated as the first duty of the state. If physical welfare were not the sole condition under which man could wake the maturity of his mind, then of itself it would in no respect deserve so much attention and regard. Man is still not very much when he lives in a warm home and has had his fill; but he has to live in a warm home and have enough to eat if his better nature is to be stirred.

This unhappy class of men uses up its best powers grappling with physical necessity; and if such men do not awaken to the light of reason they deserve more our sympathy than our scorn. But this excuse cannot be made for those freed from the yoke of necessity by a better lot, who nonetheless, and by their own choice and inclination, become slaves to their senses. What is ruled out for the former through sheer compulsion repels the latter because of their culpable lassitude. You have to summon up the courage to be wise, and for them this is too much effort. An option for enlightenment calls for daring, tearing oneself away from the comfort of idleness, harnessing all intellectual powers, forgoing many advantages with a persistence of spirit which the delicate son of pleasure finds all too difficult. They favour the twilight of dubious ideas that inspire them, and prefer their own free fantasy of the familiar and the comfortable to the bright light of a clear knowledge that drives away the favoured illusions of their dreams. Everything indefinite is quite acceptable to them, for they are freed from accommodating themselves to circumstance and imagine that they can dictate to nature. They do not flee from enlightenment because of the effort that it requires to acquire it; they fear it instead because of where it leads. They are afraid to give up treasured ideas that foster only obscurity, and of seeing both the ideas and delusions supporting the ramshackle edifice of their happiness collapse. How many men there are whose entire contentment depends upon a prejudice that will crumble at the first serious assault!

How many there are who base their entire social value upon their wealth, their forebears, their physical advantages! How many others there are who parade their supposedly great talent, dragging together what they have committed to memory, making tasteless jokes, happy in the delusion of an importance that would withstand no test. All these people would have to purchase enlightenment by sacrificing their most treasured wealth, they must face up to losing everything of which they are proud before they can taste the advantages of superior knowledge. To engage in what at first sight seems such a bad bargain they must have a gift for disavowal, a strength of mind, a decisiveness that one seldom acquires in the arms of opulence. They must set their heart upon wisdom, for it does in fact require a heartfelt commitment to give up what you already have in the hope only of future benefit.

This manliness of mind is the object of *practical* culture, and insofar as decisiveness is necessary to move from a condition of confused concepts to the most clear knowledge, then the path to theoretical culture must be opened up through practical culture. For this reason, gracious Prince, I think it right to consider the latter to be the *more urgent* need of our time, for all experience convinces me that it is not *objective* obstacles (the inadequacy of science) that are in opposition to enlightenment, so much as *subjective* obstacles (lack of willpower); that if we are still weighed down by the yoke of prejudice, then this is simply due to slackness of mind.

In maintaining that the cultivation of taste will remedy this evil, and is the most effective means to improve the faults of the age, I am far from suggesting that this is the sole means, overlooking the great part that a thorough investigation of nature and pragmatic philosophy can play in the education and cultivation of the human race. It is, however, my opinion that the unity of philosophy and experience in the enlightenment of man concerning the nature of things and his duties will be for nothing *so long as* subjective obstacles have not been cleared away, closing his senses to the knowledge of truth; and, if such knowledge does open up for him, robbing him of the capacity to behave in accordance with his new and better insight. In my view it is the work of aesthetic culture to ameliorate this fatal disposition, this work being necessarily assisted by scientific culture. Taste alone does not increase our knowledge, it does not correct our concepts, teaches us nothing about real objects. *Science* in itself is just as inadequate in remoulding our principles according to our better will, and in elevating our knowledge into *practical maxims*. Science gives us only the material for wisdom; practical maxims, on the other hand, win over our hearts, and make them our property.

Following this provisional explanation, gracious Prince, I believe I might direct your attention to the continuation of the observations I have begun included in following enclosure. Nothing is more flattering and instructive for me than your doubts; they convince me that you consider my ideas worthy of examination, and give me the opportunity to rectify their faults.

Yours etc.

Most serene Prince,

In my previous letters I have identified both extremes – a relapse into barbarism, and lassitude – as the ruling faults of our age, presenting the cultivation of taste as the most effective means of meeting this dual evil. Quite *how* a cultivated taste might bring this about, most gracious Prince, the present letter will seek to inform you; and I answer this question all the more gladly, since it gives me the opportunity of correcting a misunderstanding that quite often leads astray the judgement of philosophical minds in this matter.

Given that it is so often said that a refined feeling for beauty ennobles character and morals, it might seem superfluous to subject this material to renewed investigation. The example is invoked of the most moral of all ancient nations that, as is well known, revered beauty above all else, together with the counter-example of the barbaric peoples of both ancient and modern times who paid for their neglect of taste with a sorry degeneration. However much these examples seem to speak to the advantage of the fine arts, thinkers have more recently begun to either deny the fact, or criticize the rectitude of the conclusion. They do not find the degeneration of which uncultivated people are accused so bad, nor do they think so well of the refinement that is praised in cultivated peoples. Indeed, they go so far as to claim that the gain is not worth the sacrifice. Even in Antiquity there were men who regarded fine culture to anything but a blessing, and were for this reason inclined to refuse the arts of taste admission to their republic.

And in fact one can find barely a single example in history where aesthetic culture went hand in hand with civic virtue and political freedom. So long as Greece maintained its independence and counted among its citizens Miltiades, Aristides and Epaminondas, taste and art were still in their very early years; when, with Pericles and Alexander, the golden age of the arts arrived, Greece's virtue and liberty were already finished. We know that the Romans had first to bow down under the yoke of the Julian family before they were able to adopt Greek art, and sense the gentle influence of Gracian and the Muses. Even among the Arabs, culture did not dawn until the unlimited rule of the Abbasid Caliphate had weakened their martial spirit. In modern Italy it is known that fine art did not appear until the republican spirit was suppressed, and the glorious Lombard League had dissolved. I do not need to remind Your Serenity about the example of France, whose epoch of refinement dates from the period of its complete subjugation, and which honours Louis XIV both as the restorer of taste and as the most fearful suppressor of its liberty. Wherever we look in history we find that taste and liberty flee from one another, and that art is able to raise its throne only on the grave of heroism.

But it is usually with this energy of character that aesthetic refinement is purchased, the most effective spring of everything great and striking in man, an energy that no other greater advantage can replace. If it were really so, that the cultivation of taste would necessarily be purchased in this way, then one would be very much in the wrong to treat aesthetic culture as the instrument for promoting moral culture. Those who despise culture usually cite the enervating influence of the beautiful, denouncing the arts of taste as the worst enemy of mankind, and this complaint is often directed to the spirit of frivolity, superficiality, caprice and playfulness, qualities that are used to characterize the lover of the beautiful in thought and deed. By contrast, the beautiful world prefers to place the beneficial influence of feelings of beauty in this, its relaxing force.

> Scilicet ingenium placida mollitur ab arte
> ["'Tis in truth from the gentle art that our spirit wins tenderness']¹¹

and at another place:

> – Didicisse fideliter artes
> emollit mores nec sinit esse feros.
> [a faithful study of the liberal arts
> humanizes character and permits it not to be cruel.]¹²

And as proof of this it permits us to notice barbarian taste and crudity, with which the Graces seek revenge on their enemies. Perhaps both sides are not so far wrong, and it is not worth the trouble to reveal the basis of a dispute which has long prevented two equally respectable parties, the scholar and the world of beauty, from acknowledging the justice of the other.

The reason for this contradiction is obviously rooted in the mixed nature of man, and in the dual need that this engenders. Both parties are in dispute simply because each of them has a different *human* need in view, and their only error is that each is exclusively focussed upon one sole need. The entire contradiction dissolves once we have discovered its source.

Man, as a sensuous being, is led by impulses which work unceasingly to suppress his rational liberty, robbing him of the capacity to define himself in terms of principles. This blind power of nature in him, this merely *sensuous energy*, should be, must be, broken, and any slackening here is a necessary great step towards culture. The relaxing influence of beauty is thus without any doubt beneficial *to the extent that it takes place only in sensibility*; and the partisans of the beautiful are completely right so long as they are referring to raw natural man, or raw nature in the cultivated man.

But this softening in sensibility that the beautiful should bring about, rousing what is truly worthy in man, must not come from a lack of sensuous power, or from exhaustion; the autonomous activity of the mind must be its source, and the freedom of reason must set boundaries to the power of natural impulses. This melting and softening of which the poet talks is not at all the effect of weakness, which would deserve only scorn; it is the effect of a higher and spiritual activity: it is an action of the mind. Sense can surrender only to the mind.

This softening effect of the beautiful therefore ceases to be beneficial, becomes corrupting, *once it expresses itself in spirituality*, and those who despise this are completely right to make of this property a reproach, once they apply this to rational man.

The sensuous man cannot be sufficiently relaxed, while the rational man cannot be sufficiently exerted; everything that can be done for the cultivation of humanity follows this rule: 'to limit sensuous energy by the energy of the mind'.

If, then, aesthetic education encounters this dual need – if *on the one hand* it disarms the raw force of nature and weakens animality; if *on the other* it rouses the autonomous power of reason and realizes the truth of the mind – then it is *in this way* suited, and only *in this way*, to offer an instrument for moral education. It is this dual effect that I unrelentingly demand of culture, and the reason why it finds the necessary tools in the beautiful and the sublime.

Degeneration is countered with the beautiful, softening with the sublime, and only the most exact equilibrium of these forms of sensation perfects taste. Mere receptivity to the sublime is by no means sufficient to tear man from the state of savagery, nor can a unilateral orientation of taste to the beautiful protect him from softness. Instead, experience tends to suggest that sublime exertion of the soul, if not mitigated by feelings of beauty, fosters a degree of severity, even roughness; and that by contrast the thawing of the soul by beauty, in the absence of the sublime, ends in enervation. For the effect of the sublime is to lend tension to the soul and increase its fleetness; and it can all too easily happen that both character and emotion are reinforced, sensuous nature joining in a process of strengthening that should affect only the mind. It is for this reason that one often finds in the heroic fables of the ancient world that the most sublime virtues are linked to the most crude vices. And because the effect of the beautiful is to *thaw* the soul, then it can likewise easily happen that the primitive energy of emotions ultimately dissolves character, and spiritual nature joins in a process of relaxation that is intended only for sensuous nature. It is for this reason that one quite often finds in the refined agent the most tender feeling for harmony, beauty and order, coupled with the most disgraceful debasement of character.

Hence natural man is not in need of both the sublime and the beautiful, for he has long been moved by greatness and power before he ever begins to be sensitive to the charms of beauty. By contrast, refined man needs the sublime, for he all too willingly fritters away a power in the state of refinement that he had carried over from the state of savagery.

Most gracious Prince, it is through this distinction, which is I think founded upon reason and experience, that one can resolve the dissension encountered in the judgements of men concerning the value of aesthetic culture and its connection to moral culture, and in this way a perspective be opened up through which the relationship of taste and the arts to mankind as a whole must be evaluated. I have therefore to justify a dual claim: *firstly*, that it is the beautiful that refines the raw son of nature, and which educates the merely sensuous man into a rational one; *secondly*, that it is the sublime which compensates for the disadvantages of education in the beautiful, lending force to the refined man of art, and uniting the advantages of refinement with the virtues of savagery.

If Your Serenity finds my presentation rather too didactic, please forgive on this occasion the content, which does not permit any freer treatment without sacrificing an all-important brevity. Perhaps I will succeed in compensating for the difficult form through the inherent interest of the material, better satisfying your pure sense of truth the less that I seek to enrol your powers of imagination.

I have said that beauty helps to develop an inclination to rationality in the sensuous man. Given his duality, man is endowed with a dual inclination. Nature determines that he senses, and that he acts directly upon sensation. Reason determines that he thinks, and that he acts directly from pure thought.

I understand by nature both the causal and final connection of things; and in nature man has to prove himself as a force, and be the cause of particular effects. Generally speaking, that is his natural determination. Nature's purpose with him is directed not to *himself*, but to his effects; he entirely fulfils his natural purpose through the substance or the materiality of his action, whatever the determining cause or the formal nature of this action. Since it is generally necessary *that* something definite happens through him, *how* this actually happens is a matter of indifference for his natural purpose. Nature has secured its purposes with him by *prescribing to him through sensation* what he should bring about, allowing him to fulfil his physical determination physically, as a simple force of nature.

All natural forces are *passive* forces; they respond after they have been acted upon; and man is no different when he acts directly upon sensation, being in this respect merely a passive link in the chain of events. Nature impels mass through gravity, the organ by vegetation, animals both with reason and without by appetite and sensation.

This is true regardless of man's activity linked to a preceding need. In all such cases he merely fulfils a physical purpose and does so merely as a physical force, no matter how hyperphysical whatever it is that creates this need in him might be.

Nor are even so-called moral feelings, arising from thought and rooted in the rational part of our being, excluded from this. As sensations they are simply affections of passive force, and merely a medium of *nature* which furthers certain physical ends, such as the encouragement to activity, social association or mutual aid. When we act directly upon such sensations then it is really nature that is acting, and not ourselves as persons. And since nature requires no more of virtue than its physical consequences, it is served just as well if these physical consequences are the result of something other than virtue. Nor can nature, whose purposes are urgent, afford to wait upon our moral education (for it would have to wait a long time); instead it chooses the most certain and shortest path and *itself* secures that (through our passive power) which it cannot with any certainty expect from *us*, namely our active power. In other words: nature governs us just as much through moral sensations as through sensuous feelings, and has so governed the human race for centuries. It can do so because only the effects of our actions are of importance *for it*, and not the moral value of our actions; it *has* to do this, for it cannot suspend its purposes until we are ready to lend assistance on principle.

Nonetheless, most gracious Prince, I would not wish to be understood as if I thought little of whatever man might produce without the use of principle, or that I wished to see moral sensibility debarred from the human heart. I am in fact so far removed from such a paradox that I judge this fine capacity of the soul – to be affected by ideas of order, harmony and perfection – as a wonderful arrangement of nature, and I can never find it in myself to love the man who lacks this. Moral sensibility is for me the most effective spring in the great mechanism of humanity; but – and I must express myself clearly here – only externally, where natural necessity rules, not in our inner self, where freedom prevails. I can do no other than consider the man who possesses it as of noble nature, but for his person I have no use. To regard him highly as a *rational* being I must have previously convinced myself that he would act just as unselfishly, consistently and justly if these virtues did not have the attraction for him that they actually do, and their exercise cost as much effort as it today gives him enjoyment.

It is thus not right to found a moral distinction between these actions upon the different kinds of sensations involved in human actions. It is never the underlying mode of sensation that makes an action moral, or not moral; for what directly derives from sensation is simply physical, prescribed by nature. Inner sense, or the capacity to affect oneself through thought, *specifies* man only as an animal with a capacity for understanding and as a more noble, sensitive being; but it is only his rationality, or the capacity to act upon pure thought, that can *generically* separate him from the animal. There could be something, however intellectual, that gives him sensation; but once directly determined by this sensation, then he is determined simply as an animal with the capacity of understanding; for an animal is such for acting in this way, because it has this sensation.

I will continue my investigation, and once more beg your indulgence, most gracious Prince, for the didactic turn it has taken.

Just as the *physical* world has in view only the material aspect of my functioning, without asking after its form or causation, the *moral* world only takes the latter into account and entirely abstracts from the substance of my action, being concerned only with the form. My natural propensity is to prove myself a force within the larger context of forces, and to be the origin of particular effects. My rational propensity is to show that I am an independent and absolute force whose effect is not at all passive, but freely chosen by itself and self-determined.

Here, then, in the moral world, it is not my effect and my product that are at issue, but the productive motivation in me, my disposition. My rational propensity personifies me, since nature regards me only as a *thing*, and treats me as its *means*. The natural purpose in me runs right through and beyond me; the rational purpose in me comes to a halt at my personality, and makes *me* its centre.

Since a necessary corollary of my rational propensity is that I determine myself independently of all other conditions, it is a matter of complete indifference to this propensity how my action turns out in the sensuous world; hence nature can no longer prescribe my activity to me through sensations; instead this has to flow quite autonomously and freely from knowledge.

It is only where I act upon pure knowledge that I demonstrate absolutely free activity. In order to sense I must place something outside of myself that defines my condition: *I have a need*. This is not so when I think or perceive; for if I can only express my greatest capacity for thought as if it were nothing more than matter that ultimately has to come from outside of me, then it does not originate in this matter, but only there becomes visible. Thought is an operation that I perform with my thought-matter; sensation is a passion inflicted upon me by matter. If a sensation determines my action, then the cause of my activity lies *outside* of myself, and I *receive* what is decreed. If on the other hand knowledge determines my action, the cause of my activity is *within* me, and I *give myself* the law. Sensuousness is a state of dependence, rationality is a state of freedom.

And so from this servitude of nature I should raise myself up to the worthiness of the spirits, of mankind, of deity. My moral propensity simply requires that I be capable of abstracting from all sensation whenever reason, my supreme legislator, so demands. But I was a sensuous being long before I became aware of being an intelligence, and although reason has a moral *priority* within me, the nature in me does have a physical *advance*. Before the autonomous mind has checked its powers impulse has taken control. So should I, once moral knowledge is aroused, quit my accustomed habit, and deploy a power with whose use I am unpractised against that which had hitherto been my sole resort. How, then, will I find a way from this sensuous dependence to moral freedom.

In this state of spiritual nakedness could perhaps the skill that I acquired during my sensuous functioning be of any use? If I could expect assistance from *nature*, then the transition would not be so difficult. But it is for exactly that reason that the rational freedom of action exists: that all natural influences cease, and absolute and entire abstraction made from everything sensuous. Matter can simply not be permitted to intervene in the pure dictate of reason if the idea of pure dictate is not to be abrogated; and so there is no other way of making a transition possible than by involving the autonomous action of reason with the affairs of sensuousness. If the moral procedures of the soul do not allow themselves to be sensualized, then sensuous procedures must be rationalized. In short: if matter is neither permitted to climb nor capable of climbing up to the mind, then the mind has to come down to matter.

It is quite simply necessary that man, where he has to legitimate himself as an intelligent being, must demonstrate pure autonomy; but it is not really necessary that, where he acts as a sensuous being, he acts *only as such*, behaving only in a passive manner. On the contrary: as much as it shames man to accomplish through passivity what he should have done actively, so it honours and uplifts him to do with the assistance of active powers what ordinary souls could only do with passive. My regard for a man shrinks once I see him reaching for material incentives where his duty and obligation are quite distinct (even if these incentives are founded religiously). My estimation of someone rises if he shows taste where another would simply satisfy his needs.

Hence in the domain of sensations our autonomous spirit must disclose its effectiveness, *setting to work* a power in sensuous affairs that should, subsequently, enter the moral domain in complete purity. We can note three distinct eras or degrees, if you like, through which man has to pass before he becomes what nature and reason have determined for him.

At the first stage he is no more than a passive power. Here he just senses what nature external to him allows him to feel, and he defines himself only according to the way that he feels. He feels passion, because matter is given to him from outside; and he feels aversion simply because nothing is given to him, or has been taken from him. Either *he* seizes objects and wants to devour them, out of pure desire; or the objects overwhelm him, and he pushes them away, in detestation. In this oppressive dependence on natural conditions man vegetates until, at the second stage, contemplation makes him free.

A liking for contemplation is the first *liberal* relationship of man to the natural world. If need seizes its object directly, so contemplation moves its own into the distance. Desire destroys its object, contemplation does not touch it. The natural forces that before had so oppressively and alarmingly intruded upon the slave of sensuousness now give way before free contemplation, and space is created between man and the phenomenon. If the boorish reveller gloats at the sight of a female beauty, he is always (if not in fact, then in imagination) thinking of possession, of immediate pleasure. If the man of taste is captivated by the same sight, then for him mere contemplation is enough. He wants nothing from the object itself and, satisfied with the mere idea, he is indifferent to her existence; and at the very least, his pleasure has nothing in common with that of the former.

Indeed, I too behave passively when sensing beauty, as in quite material pleasures, to the extent that I receive the impression of the one or the other externally, and this impression puts me in a state of pleasure. But, with a beautiful object, the pleasure in this impression does not come from outside – it is not a material impression upon my capacity for sensation, but instead an intervening operation of my soul: of reflection upon what places me in a state of pleasure. Material pleasure derives directly from matter that I receive; aesthetic liking comes from the form I lend matter I have received. I delight in pleasant things, because it gives me the opportunity to *suffer* something; I delight in the beautiful because it gives me the opportunity to *do* something.

A liking for free contemplation allows me to relate objects no longer merely to my physical condition, but directly to my reason, and to influence my passive capacity directly by my active. I behave passively insofar as I feel sensation; but I feel sensation only because I was active. I do receive, although I do so not from a natural mechanism, but from the power of thought.

My liking for free contemplation has therefore opened up my rationality without having discarded my sensuousness. I have gained the important experience that I am more, and have more in me, than merely passive power; and I have begun to exercise this higher power. To begin with I was nothing but an instrument upon which physical necessity played. I felt, because something happened to me; because I felt, I desired. Cause and effect were here purely physical. Now, at the second stage, I involve myself as a free principle and as a person in my condition. I still suffer passively, for I feel, but I suffer because I have acted. Here the effect is physical (feeling, sensation), but the cause of this sensation is not . It is not external matter that affects my capacity to feel, but internal matter, an idea born of reason. One further step and I act because I acted; I want to do something because I registered something. I elevate concepts into ideas, and ideas to practical maxims. Here, at the third stage, I leave sensuousness entirely behind me, and have elevated myself to the freedom of pure spirits.

(The common saying that extremes converge is also entirely right here, for as soon as we abstract from the content of two opposing forms of a soul's constitution – the condition of extreme dependence and the condition of extreme freedom – they follow exactly the same rule. The entirely rational and the entirely sensuous man share in common the fact that they are both *directly* determined, the latter by sensation and the former by pure knowledge. The same rigidity with which nature dominates the slave of the senses is practised by moral law with respect to moral will; the same laxity that the sensuous man allows the laws of mind is allowed by the reason of the moral man with regard to the laws of nature. Right or wrong – passion dictates that I must take my pleasure. 'Fiat justitia et pereat mundus', says duty).[13]

The capacity to sense the beautiful thus creates a bond between the sensuous and spiritual nature of man, preparing the soul for its transition from a condition of pure passivity to the unconditional autonomy of reason. Beauty *introduces* the freedom of the intellect into the world of sense, and the pure daimonic flame (if you will permit me the metaphor) allows its ethereal colours to play upon the mirror of matter as the light of the day does on dawn's clouds.[14]

This reminds me of a passage from my poem 'The Artists', which, I no longer know why, was replaced by another. It can be placed here as a ruin:

> With what lustre the clouds mill,
> and the mountain's sunlit peak burns,
> before it, the Queen of radiance
> lights up the firmament;
> the goddess of beauty dances lightly dressed
> before the golden day of knowledge
> and the youngest of the heavenly choir
> opens for her the pathway of light.

Thursday, 21 November 1793, Ludwigsburg

Most serene Prince,

Before leaving the material that I have begun, please allow
me to demonstrate historically what I have so far developed
only theoretically. I will go back to primeval times, and follow
the first few steps towards humanity that an infant mankind
makes.

What was man before he was taken in hand by the art of
making souls? The most stubborn egoist among all the animal
species; and while inclined to freedom, the most dependent of
slaves to his senses. He had regard only for himself and had no
time for anything that did not quell his crude desires. Beauteous
nature spread her wonders before him for naught. He saw nothing in nature save booty with which he could sate his greed. He
looked upon the bounties of nature only with the covetousness
of a thief, and when nature showed its grandeur and power
in thunder, earthquakes and floods, man responded with the
servility of a malefactor. He concerned himself only with indis-
criminate and direct satisfaction. The sexual impulse was all that
bound him to his spouse, and the satisfaction of this impulse
was all that he asked of her. In his clothing, in his equipage and
his home, he attended only to the barest necessity. A cave was
enough to protect him from the depredations of wild animals
and the weather. If he lacked a cave, then he made an artificial
one from branches or stones; however miserable it might be, it
was good enough for bare necessity. As stubborn as he was in
the face of his own weakness, he was pusillanimous in the face
of higher powers. He laid claim to everything that he could

overcome; anything for which his strength was no match was a foe directed against him; he attributed to everything that presented itself before him the same murderous selfishness that he harboured in his own breast.

This is how wretched man seems to us at his earliest stage. This is how Thucydides describes the ancient Pelasgians,[15] and those voyaging the world have confirmed his descriptions for many peoples of the South Seas and northern Asia.

I now quit this depressing vista, most gracious Prince, so as to present a more happy one. What kind of phenomenon was it that sparked the humanization of these wild tribes? However many historical accounts we might refer to, it is for all peoples the same: a love of finery.

The savage ceases to be satisfied with bare necessity; he asks that it has another property: a property that no longer satisfies his animal impulses, but a need for a better lineage. This property is the beautiful. Of course, beautiful only in relation to his savage taste, but this is not a matter of *content*, but only of the *form of judgement*; and this brings about a change. It is no longer founded upon direct material sensation, but on reflection, upon free contemplation. Even if something ugly is judged to be beautiful it demonstrates the activity of a free capacity to express a liking without sensuous interest, the beginning of taste, even if it is still grotesque.

For the savage, the beautiful is the unusual, something that stands out, something colourful. He makes grotesque figurines, loves bright colours and shrill music. But since these qualities cannot improve his material well-being, one must assume that he relates them to his power for thought, and values them not because he is directly made aware of something pleasant, but because they touch him directly as inducements to activity. Subjectively, therefore, they belong to the family 'beautiful', no matter how much they might be excluded from it objectively. They suit his inner sense, since they stir his intellect into activity.

Now the savage begins to pay attention to the impression that he makes upon others. *He wants to be liked*. Just this first impulse makes him a man. He could not have this need had he not begun to leave the narrow bounds of necessity, and make use of a measure for the value of things distinct from its relation to his own pleasure. Everything that he possesses must now fulfil a requirement additional to the service it provides. It must stand out, and appeal to the eye; this is how taste first emerges. Having at the first stage simply pleased himself, he now begins to choose; and this choice is guided by something that is of greater value than his entire previous existence. Now the ancient German looks for better-looking animal skins, more imposing antlers, more delicate drinking cups; the North Caledonian lays on the most colourful shellfish for his feasts. Even weapons are no longer simple instruments of terror, but also something pleasing to the eye. The rough yells of the field take on a rhythm, and begin to turn into song.

Being unsatisfied with beautifying necessaries, the savage-turned-man makes beauty an end in itself, and wants particular things simply on this account. He adorns himself. The objects of his desire increase, the number of his goods grows, until artificial needs outweigh his natural needs. Mere use is already too narrow a bound for his expanded inclinations. He decorates his hair with feathers, his neck with coral shells, he even decorates his own body, and in seeking to beautify himself distorts his natural form to a hideous degree. In this way he introduces into his social conduct and his morals flourishes and embellishments, showing a liking for moving beyond considerations of utility in seeking to satisfy the impulse for free pleasure that has been aroused in him. However much these early attempts to move away from the simplicity of nature might seem quixotic, tasteless and nonsensical, they are so precisely because they involve a move away from nature, the effects of a capacity to more freely develop oneself; they are, therefore, the first registration of free reason and so worthy of some acknowledgement. They prove to us that these individual persons and peoples in which we encounter this development have survived the era of complete tutelage and the rule of nature; that they are no longer savages, but *barbarians*; for savagery means the complete lack of human development, while barbarism is improper human development.

A very advantageous change in the relationship between the genders now becomes apparent. No longer is it solely blind natural impulse that brings them together. Attractiveness is demanded of the woman, effort from the man, and beauty is the reward of bravery. Freedom expresses itself in the work of instinct, and since instinct is not otherwise guided by volition, this expression of freedom is a clear and open proof that something higher than nature was here at work.

Social intercourse also takes on a quite different appearance. More dependent on the good opinion of others, since he wants to be liked, the crude egoist must master the impetuosity of his emotion, and respect the freedom beyond himself, since he also wants to please freedom. So long as he is only in a physical relationship with others he can be an object only of a self-seeking impulse to self-preservation, and never of free aesthetic judgement. He must therefore quit the inimical and warlike state of nature and transform himself into an object of selfless and calm contemplation. However, this is possible only if he himself becomes charitable; if he no longer confronts others as an enemy, if he does not disturb their self-love through impulsive and forceful expression; in short, if he does not, like a hostile star, drag others into the turmoil of his *existence*, but deals with them like a distantly twinkling star, purely as a nice idea.

However, nothing reveals the beneficial transformation in manner of feeling more clearly than the cheerful and laughing form that religion and morals assume after the impulse for beauty has been aroused. Fear is the spirit of all worship before taste sets souls free. Gods and demons declare themselves to the childlike age of mankind through their power, and for the slave to needs, everything powerful is at once awful. Servile lamentation marks his devotions, his divine worship is sombre and quite often fearful. Once, however, the sense for beauty is aroused, and a despondent impulse of self-preservation is no longer the exclusive standard of judgement, then ideas of the gods also improve, and man enters into a more refined relationship with them. Since they no longer burst upon him as pure natural forces, he gains the space to fix them with the calm gaze of contemplation. The spectral forms with which the gods had terrorized his childhood are discarded, and he is surprised by the sight of a refined version of himself. The divine monster of the Orient ruling the world with the blind strength of a predator merges in Greek fantasy with the amicable form of mankind, and even the father of the gods has to exchange his clumsy and titanic power for beauty to win the favour of one of his peoples, whom only form, and no longer simple matter, can satisfy.

And so the silent power of beauty gradually subdues raw nature, initiating the savage into manhood, and teaching him how he might, even in his physical condition of slavery, seek his daimonic liberty. But its benevolent effects are not limited to rendering sensations spiritual, preparing long in advance pure spirituality. Its influence on the latter is closer and more direct, for even in its absolutely free activity, in the work of knowledge and in choice, it supports the spirit against the resistance of sensuousness, even though it can play no positive part in this work.

The investigation of truth calls for abstraction and a rigorous conformity, which the indolence and caprice of the senses resist. Concentration of the power of thought is also needed, so that form, which alone contains truth, might be separated from matter. To win over for the pure activity of reason a sensuous capacity which always holds fast to matter, vanquishing its resistance, it is necessary to convert form back into matter, to cloak ideas in intuition, and to work upon passive power with active power. Only in this way, even with the pure work of knowledge in sensuousness, can any gain be made, replacing work with pleasure, exertion with relaxation, activity with passivity.

This is what taste does in the cause of truth. With beauty, reason begins to mix its regularity with the capricious play of imagination. With beauty, imagination and powers of sensation begin to receive more refined material from reason, becoming interested in the increased activity of the soul. Beauty does not therefore merely serve to raise sense to the power of thought, and transform play into seriousness; it also helps to bring the power of thought to the senses, and transform seriousness into play. The first of these two is gained by taste from the *sensible* part of the world, the second from the *thinking* part.

It is known that man is called upon to think only through the stimulus of pleasure, provided the strong impulses of his natural indolence do not intervene; and this pleasure has to follow immediately from his activity itself, and not from the consequences of such activity. The anticipated consequences of his activity – whether they mostly flow from it, like insight from reflection, or coincidentally combine with it, like the wage with work, or fame with skill – can never serve as generally effective stimuli, for whether we have an idea of it, whether we have hopes of it, and whether we place value upon it – these always remain problematic. Something very great that we anticipate can, if it is sufficiently enticing, spur us on to work, while not hiding the present trouble such effort requires, nor the feeling of compulsion. If this latter feeling is to be completely expunged from the soul pleasure must follow exertion so quickly that consciousness of the two conditions can barely be distinguished. A master of presentation must therefore possess the skill necessary to transform in the blink of an eye the work of abstraction into material for the imagination, turn concepts into images, dissolve conclusions into feelings and conceal the strict regularity of the intellect beneath a veneer of caprice.

In very few cases does intellect work *logically*, that is, with a clear consciousness of the rules and principles which guide it; in the vast majority of cases it works aesthetically, and as a form of rhythm, as Your Serenity has already seen from the use of language, introducing into all languages for this kind of intellect the expression *common sense*.[16] It is not that sense could ever think; intellect works just as well here as in the schooled thinker, it is just that the rules to which he adheres are not held in his consciousness, and that in such a case it is not the operation of intellect itself, only its effect upon our condition that we experience as pleasure or displeasure. Before the soul has taken the time to be its own observer, and give due account of its procedure, the inner sense is affected, action turns to passivity, and thought to sensation.

To serve the metre of this interplay the orator or writer of taste must *realize* his work, although he would be very much in the wrong to create it only *by means of* this metre. If, on the other hand, he also realizes his work in terms of the logical understanding through which he had conceived it, he shifts the work of production which he should have done himself to each of his hearers or listeners; he detains them longer than sense would like in the enforced condition of abstraction, while delaying the far more preferable condition of perception and sensation. And so he does them a kind of violence, and is disliked because he offends their freedom.

I need not add, most gracious Prince, that this law of taste is subjected to ideas directed to conversation and persuasion, and not the kind of endeavours expressly devoted to rigorous proof and which are intended to convince. These latter are not only liberated from all demands of taste, taste is even in conflict with their aim, to excel in respect of the aesthetic; for the condition of pleasure is unfavourable to proof, and a tasteful treatment of logical machinery conceals that upon which all philosophical conviction is based. Kant's *Critique of Reason*[17] would clearly be a rather less complete work if it had been written with more taste. Such a writer would not reasonably expect to interest readers who did not share his purpose.

By contrast, he who *wishes* to be generally pleasing is excused by no subject-matter, he has to respect the freedom of imagination, he must conceal the logical apparatus by which he guides the intellect of his reader. If a didactic lecture runs in a straight line with hard corners, proceeding with mathematical rigour, the fine lecture moves forward with a wave-like motion, at each point changing course unnoticed, coming back to the same point unremarked. One could say that the *didactic* teacher forces his concepts upon us; the *Socratic* teacher draws them out of us; while the orator and poet lend us the opportunity of creating them ourselves in a seemingly free manner.

In the same way that a tasteful lecture prompts thought, and moves knowledge towards truth because it forms material for sensibility from abstract concepts, so taste assists in furthering the *morality of action*, bringing into agreement the moral precepts of reason and the interest of the senses, transforming the idea of virtue into an object of inclination.

But here, most gracious Prince, I enter into a territory in which it is as dangerous as it is easy to commit a misstep; I therefore see myself forced to slow my pace. There are very many thinkers who wish to know nothing about the influence of taste on morality, and in this domain there are far more who fear this than hope for it. In the following letters I will have the opportunity to examine their arguments.

Permit me, in the hope that the interest of Your Serenity in these exchanges might not diminish to the same degree as my interest in them increases, to continue onward.

Yours etc.

Most serene Prince,

Today I take up my pen with mixed feelings of perplexity and courage. I must answer the question, *how much does virtue take from taste*; and fear that I will in so doing fall into a more serious tone that is even less suited to written communication than the tone I have previously employed. Nonetheless, I do remember to whom I am writing, and although today's choice of object might offend the delicate sensibilities of the man of the world, I will find all the more support in the heart of the friend of virtue, and in the love of truth of the philosophical thinker who is indifferent to no object of investigation.

I must confess straight away that I am thoroughly Kantian in my thinking about the principal parts of moral philosophy. I believe, and am convinced, that only those of our actions can be called *moral* which involve a simple respect for the law of reason; and not those involving impulses, however refined they may be, whatever imposing names they might go under. In agreement with the most strict moralists, I believe that virtue is simply something for itself, and can be related to none of its various purposes. The good is – according to Kantian principles, which I completely endorse – what happens because it is good.

If I attribute to taste the merit of contributing to the promotion of morality, it can in no way be my intention to claim that the part that good taste plays in an action renders this action moral. The moral can have no other basis than itself. Taste can *favour* the morality of conduct, as I hope to demonstrate in this letter, but it cannot through its influence *create* something moral.

Here it is exactly the same with inner and moral freedom as it is with external and physical freedom. I act freely in the latter sense if I simply follow my own will, independently of any alien influence. But it can be that I owe the possibility of following my own will in an unconstrained manner to a reason distinct from my own, once it is assumed that this latter could have constrained my will. In the same way, my possibility of acting for good might be owed to a cause distinct from my reason, once this last is conceived as a force which is capable of limiting the freedom of my soul. In the same way that one can say than a person can *receive* freedom from another, even though freedom consists in man being relieved of any need to conduct himself in accordance with others, so one can just as well say that taste *provides assistance to* virtue, even though virtue expressly implies that it requires no external assistance.

An action in no respect ceases to be free because, quite fortunately, he who might have been able to constrain it abstained from so doing; it is free once we know that the actor merely follows his own will without regard to anyone or anything else. In the same way, an inner action does not cease deserving to be called a moral action because of the fortunate absence of temptation that might have nullified its morality; it deserves to be called a moral action once we assume that the actor follows an expression of his reason, excluding all alien motivations. The freedom of an external action rests upon its *direct origin in the will of the person*; the morality of an inner action rests merely on the *direct determination of the will through the law of reason*.

I beg your indulgence, Serenity, in developing this analogy. It can be easier or more difficult to act as free men, according to the contrary forces that we encounter, and to which we must bend. To this extent there are degrees of freedom. Our freedom is greater, visibly greater at least, when we uphold it against the powerful resistance of an inimical force; but it does not cease to exist if our will encounters no such resistance, or if an alien power intervenes and destroys this resistance without any action of our own.

It is just the same with morality. It can cost us a greater or lesser amount of struggle to adhere directly to reason, insofar as impulses stir within us that are contrary to its precepts and which we have to reject. To this extent there are degrees of morality. Our morality is the greater, or at least more prominent, when we conform directly to reason, even when impulses to do the opposite are at their strongest; but it does not for this reason cease when it encounters no contrary stimulus, or if something other than our free will neutralizes these stimuli. It is enough to say that, when we act morally, we act morally because it is moral, without first asking ourselves whether it is pleasant – presuming it highly likely that we would behave differently if it caused us pain, or withdrew a pleasure.

It can be said to the honour of human nature that no man can sink so low as to favour evil just because it is evil; rather that all, without distinction, would favour the good because it is good if it did not accidentally rule out something pleasant, or instead brought something unpleasant in its train. In reality, all immorality seems to come from the collision of the good with the pleasant, or what comes to the same thing, of desire with reason; being rooted also on the one hand in the strength of *sensuous* impulses, and on the other in the *weakness* of moral will. Morality can therefore be furthered in two ways, just like it can be obstructed in two ways. Either one has to strengthen the part played by reason and the strength of good will so that no temptation can overwhelm them; or the power of temptation must be broken, so that a weaker reason and a weaker good will might still have the advantage.

It could, of course, seem as though morality itself would gain nothing from the last operation, for there is no alteration to the will, whose sole role it is to ensure that all action is moral. But in the example above, this is not at all the case where we have only a good will that is weak, and not an imperfect will that one would have to change. And this weak good will does in this way have an effect, which perhaps would not have happened if it had been confronted with strong impulses. Where, however, good will becomes the basis of an action, it can be said that morality is truly present.

I have therefore no reservations, most gracious Prince, in stating the principle that whatever destroys an inclination contrary to the good truly furthers morality.

The most dangerous inner foe of morality is the sensuous impulse, which seeks satisfaction as soon as something is presented to it, and as soon as reason bids it do something objectionable sets itself against all precepts of reason. This sensuous impulse works unceasingly to draw the will into its interest; the will being governed by moral laws, with the obligation of never finding itself in conflict with reason. But the sensuous impulse recognizes no such moral law, and wants to have its object realized through the will, whatever reason might have to say about it. This tendency of our appetite to dictate directly to our will without any regard for higher laws conflicts with our moral determination, and is the strongest opponent with which man in his moral action has to contend.

Raw and uncouth souls lack both moral and aesthetic education, allow pure appetite to dictate to them, behaving merely as their desire leads them. Moral souls who lack aesthetic education allow reason to dictate to them, and it is only through respect for their duty that they triumph over their temptations. In aesthetically refined souls there is a further item that quite often replaces virtue where it is lacking, and aids it where it is already present.

This item is taste. Taste furthers moderation and decency, it abhors everything that is awkward, blunt and violent, and favours everything that flows together simply and harmoniously. And that in the storm of sensation we still hear the voice of reason, and place a limit on the irruptions of nature – we already know that this demands an etiquette, which itself is nothing other than an aesthetic law, of every civilized man. This constraint that the civilized man places upon himself in expressing his emotions creates for him a degree of command over these emotions, providing for him at least the ability to interrupt the passive condition of his soul with an act of autonomy, halting through reflection the hasty transition of feelings into actions. However, all that the blind force of emotions breaks creates no virtue (for this has to be its own work); but it does create space for the will to turn towards virtue.

Taste can therefore be seen as the first weapon used by an aesthetic soul in its struggle against raw nature, driving back this assault before it becomes necessary for reason to intervene as a legislator, and pronounce judgement. This victory of taste over pure emotion is, however, not any kind of moral action, and the freedom that the will acquires here through the action of taste is not any kind of moral freedom. Here taste merely liberates the soul from the yoke of instinct so that it might lay on *its own* fetters, and by disarming the first open enemy of moral freedom, it can happen that it becomes the second such enemy, which, under the cloak of friendship, can be all the more dangerous. And so taste governs the soul only through the stimulus of pleasure – a noble pleasure, certainly, since reason is its source – but where pleasure determines the will there is no morality: one set of chains has simply been exchanged for another.

Something important is, however, gained by this intervention of taste in the operation of the will. All of those material inclinations and crude desires that so often oppose the good so violently and stubbornly are expelled from the soul by taste, implanting there instead more refined and gentle inclinations related to order, harmony and perfection; and if these are not in themselves virtues, they do share *one* object with virtue. If now desire is expressed, then it must first undergo strict examination by the sense of beauty; and if reason now expresses itself, demanding actions related to order, harmony and perfection, not only does it encounter no resistance, but it also instead receives the lively and vivacious applause of nature.

If we review the various forms in which morality can express itself, we can without any difficulty reduce them all to these two. Either sensuousness (nature) sets the soul in motion, so that something either happens, or does not happen, the will governing according to the law of reason; or reason sets the soul in motion, and will is obedient to it, without consulting the senses.

The Greek princess Anna Komnene has told of a captive rebel whom her father Alexius, while the general of his predecessor, had the task of escorting to Constantinople.[1] On the

way, riding together, Alexius was seized by the desire to halt
in the shadow of a tree to gain some respite from the heat of
the sun. Very soon he was overcome by sleep, while the other,
constantly fearing his imminent death, remained awake. While
Alexius was still sleeping, the prisoner saw his escort's sword
hanging from a branch, and he became tempted to free himself through murder. Anna Komnene suggested that she did not
know what would have happened if Alexius had not just then
fortunately woken up. Here, most gracious Prince, is a moral
action of the first kind, in which the sensuous impulse makes
the first move, and then acknowledges reason as judge. Had the
prisoner conquered temptation simply out of regard for justice,
there would be no doubt that he had acted morally.

When the late Duke Leopold of Brunswick approached the
banks of the River Oder in full spate, and asked for advice
on whether he should risk his life to cross the stormy flood to
save some unfortunates who would be helpless without him –
and when he, driven solely (as I suppose) by a sense of duty,
jumped into a boat that no one else would enter, no one seeking to dissuade him could be said to have acted morally.[19]
The duke found himself in the opposite situation to the
preceding case. The idea of duty had priority, the impulse to
self-preservation only then stirring to resist the movement of
reason. However, in both cases the will behaved in the same
way: it adhered to reason, and so both instances are moral.

But would both cases remain so if we allowed taste to play
a role?

Assuming that the first, the prisoner who was tempted to
commit a bad act and failed to do so out of respect for justice,
has such cultivated taste that everything disgraceful and violent prompts a degree of abhorrence in him that nothing can
overcome, then at the very moment that a natural impulse stirs
his inclination it will be rejected simply by taste. It will never be
brought before the moral tribunal of conscience, but be dealt
with by a prior control. Here, however, taste governs the will
only by feelings, not through laws. The prisoner denies himself
the pleasant feeling of his own life saved because he cannot
bear the horrible feeling of having done something vile. All

of this therefore takes place in the forum of sensation, and in the domain of passivity, and the conduct of this man, however legal it is, is morally neutral; simply a benign effect of nature.

Taking now the second case, where reason directed that something had to be done quite against natural impulse; assume that this man has just as sensitive a sense of beauty delighted by everything that is impressive and perfect. At the same moment that reason expresses itself sensibility will join with it, and he will be *positively* inclined to do that which, in the absence of this gentle receptiveness to beauty, would have been *contrary to* his inclination. Would you therefore, most gracious Prince, consider the second case to be any less perfect than the first? Certainly not, because in the first as much as in the second the protagonist follows the dictate of reason, and the fact that he follows this dictate with pleasure makes no difference to the moral purity of his act. The second is just as perfect *morally* as the first; *physically*, on the other hand, he is much more perfect, since he is *a much more* fitting subject for virtue.

Taste therefore provides the soul with a useful disposition to virtue by removing the natural causes that obstruct it, and arouses those that are favourable to it. Taste cannot diminish in any way true virtue, for in all cases where the natural impulse makes the first move taste brings before its tribunal that which conscience would have had to present; and it therefore causes the actions of those who are governed by it to be much more indifferent to morality than true to it. For the sublimity of men is not at all based upon the greater number of moral actions, but on the greater capacity of the soul to effect such actions; indeed, perhaps in the era of the fulfilled moral ideal we will hear as little about morality and moral deeds as in the golden era of nature and of childhood, and be reminded only in the most unusual cases that it is reason and not inclination that guides us. By contrast, taste can make positive use of virtue in all those cases where reason makes the first move, and is in danger of being overruled by the eloquence of nature. In such cases taste defines our sensibility to the advantage of duty, and renders even a small degree of moral willpower capable of exercising virtue.

If, therefore, taste in no respect harms true morality, and in several cases clearly makes use of it, that it very much promotes the *legality* of our conduct assumes great importance.

Assuming that fine culture does absolutely nothing to lend us greater conviction, it does at least provide us with the skill, in the absence of truly moral conviction, to act as we would have done if we did have moral conviction. Before a moral forum, our conduct is of no concern whatsoever, except insofar as it is an expression of our convictions; conversely, before a physical forum and the realm of nature our convictions are of no concern, except insofar as they give rise to actions that further the aims of nature.

Both world orders, the physical world governed by powers and the moral world governed by laws, are so closely linked, so intricately bound up with one another, that actions are morally useful in their form, and also include within themselves a physical purposiveness; in the same way that the entire construction of nature seems to exist in order to make possible the highest of all purposes, the good, so the good allows itself to be used as a means to preserve this construction. The order of nature is therefore made dependent upon the morality of our convictions, and we cannot offend against the moral world without at the same time causing confusion in the physical world.

If, so long as human nature remains as it is, it can never ever be expected to behave uniformly and consistently as a pure spiritual nature without interruption or backsliding; never to offend against moral order by finding itself in contradiction with the precepts of reason – if, however much we are convinced of both the necessity and the possibility of pure virtue, we have to admit to ourselves how really accidental the exercise of pure virtue is, and how little we may rely on the invincibility of our best principles – if, being conscious of our unreliability, we keep in mind that the edifice of nature suffers from every one of our moral lapses; if we keep all of this in mind, then it would be the most frivolous boldness to allow the best for the world to depend upon the approximation of our virtue. Instead, there is here an obligation laid upon us to ensure that the substance of our actions meets the demands of the physical world, even if we are not capable of properly creating the moral world through our moral actions; at least, as a more complete instrument to pay what we owe as imperfect persons for natural ends, so that we do not bring disgrace into both world orders at once. If, because they have no moral value, we do not wish to for any institutions in respect of the legality of our conduct, then all the bonds of society could be torn apart by the time we are done with our principles. The more accidental our morality, the more necessary it is to make arrangements for legality, and a casual or arrogant infringement of the latter would be met with a moral reckoning for us. In the same way that the madman who senses a paroxysm coming on voluntarily clears away all knives and offers himself up to be bound, so that he might not be responsible while in a healthy condition for the crimes of his sick brain – so are we also obliged to bind ourselves, while free, through religion and aesthetic virtue, so that when our passion is in full flood it does not rage against the world order.

I have not here placed religion and taste together in one class unintentionally, for both have the merit of being a surrogate for true virtue, securing the regularity of actions where there is no hope of the obligation of conviction. Although there is no doubt that he for whom neither the charms of beauty nor belief in providence and immortality *were needed* in order to act in all cases in accordance with duty would be deserving of a higher place in the spiritual world, nonetheless, the familiar limitations of mankind compelled even the most strict ethicist to relax somewhat the rigour of his system *in its application*, if at the same time he felt unable to condone the same *in theory*, and make fast the well-being of a world that would be ill-served by the accidental nature of our virtue with the two strong anchors of religion and taste.

And indeed both seem, if I might otherwise trust my own experience, to divide themselves in men and in the human species *in such a way* that religion opens its arms to those upon whom beauty is lost. Where no aesthetic culture has opened up the inner sense, calmed the outer, and where the more noble sensations of the intellect and the heart have not yet restricted the ordinary needs of the senses; or in situations where even the greatest refinement of taste cannot prevent the sensuous impulse from seeking material satisfaction – for it is religion that assigns an object to the sensuous impulse, securing for that impulse compensation for the sacrifice that it brings to virtue. We are all part of this, with the difference only that the raw man is in this situation permanently, while the refined man is only there for a moment.

A soul that has begun to enjoy a more refined pleasure in forms, and has begun to take its pleasures from the pure source of reason, relinquishes without a struggle the common pleasures of matter, and considers itself compensated for the privation of external sense by the pleasures of inner sense. But there is one case where we all, whether raw or refined, revert to the power of instinct, and where nature, despite all art, reigns supreme. No aesthetic culture goes so far that it could rebuff the natural impulse where it reacts against *life and existence*. All that taste can do is to *alter* the object of our desire, and *exchange* our more crude sensations for more refined ones. So long as reason, in exercising its legislative moral function, merely requires the sacrifice of individual sensations, taste is able to provide to inner sense what has been taken away from the outer; but once reason itself demands the sacrifice *of power itself*, and touches upon the ultimate cause of everything, even mental sensation, then taste has nothing more to replace, because, as one half sensuous capacity, it sees itself embroiled in the fate of sense, and together with its existence *its* rule is also at an end. Where the capacity of sensation ceases there can be no exchange of sensations, and all that remains is the suppression of an impulse that we can no longer satisfy. This can, however, be done only through the most violent of all abstractions and through an expression of strength of which the mixed nature of man is scarcely capable. This would require a leap from the conditional into the unconditional, and a complete renunciation of everything in us that was part of matter and was governed by natural conditions, hence of existence, consciousness and effect. Merely the pure form of reason, cloaked in its unchangeable identity, and separated from all matter, would remain, and even the idea of the absolute and the necessary would be included in the general loss, since it cannot be conceived without temporal determination and material. Since for this operation of the soul a strength is needed of which only the smallest number of men are capable, and such men even then only at their best, we would do well to keep religious ideas in reserve for this most extreme event, so that we might be able to secure satisfaction for the ineluctable life impulse in another order of things. Should I speak freely, most gracious Prince? Religion is for the sensuous man what taste is to the refined man; taste is for everyday life what religion is for the extreme. Given that we are not gods, we *must* call a halt at one of these two supports, if not rather at both.

Even a passing glance at the contemporary moral constitution of the world confirms for me my observations. Consider the mass of the people: its religion is the counterweight to its passions where there is no external resistance to break their strength. The common man would forbid himself much as a *Christian* that he would as a *man* have allowed himself. If we consider the finer classes, they have good manners, but are not moral. The rules of decency, of good form and of honour are sufficient to keep them from infringing laws that they are a very long way from observing. If interest would be too weak a bridle for them, then it is taste that assures us of the regularity of their conduct. I do not doubt that there are among both classes examples of true virtue, but I very much fear that they are the exception, and not the rule. In France a convulsion has now both overthrown religion and sacrificed taste to brutalization, and much is missing in the formation of the character of the nation to dispense with these pillars. Time will tell how things will turn out.

Might I, most excellent Prince, hope for your forgiveness in regard to the free expression with which I have ended this letter? I admit that it was also here my purpose to reveal to you what kind of person I am, since before those whom I respect and love to this degree I would wish to present myself complete and unadorned, as from my own heart.

Yours etc.

December 1793, Ludwigsburg

Most serene Prince,

In the preceding letters I have sought to demonstrate that the sense of the beautiful serves to support true virtue, where this is absent replacing it with the sense of the aesthetic. This aesthetic virtue, although it acquires for man no value in the moral world, renders him nonetheless viable in the physical world, making him capable of a regularity of conduct without which nature could never achieve its great aim of uniting men into a whole. But men are still a long way from being united when they have ceased disputing among themselves, and legality alone can prevent injustice tearing the bonds of society. To unite men truly and inwardly requires another, positive bond, that of social character, or the communication of sensations, and the exchange of ideas.

Mere need can bring men together into society, but only taste can make them sociable; while necessity can develop man's dual nature, it is only beauty that can unite this nature. Taste alone introduces a harmonic unity into society, because it engenders a harmonic unity in the individual.

Regard for the communicability of sensations and ideas is, of course, the first law that dictates a good tone to all the members of a civilized society. Good tone proscribes everything that excludes. It demands that all, without distinction, should have their part in what the one understands, and another feels.

But the pleasures of the senses that are founded upon direct sensation and a material cause, and the completely contrasting pure intellect related to abstraction and logical forms, have in common with each other that neither is capable of pure communication. The former because they are oriented to individual sensibility and private needs, which are accidental; the latter not because they arise from an unchangeable and communal disposition of the intellect, but because they follow from the special application and development of this disposition – which is likewise accidental, and which cannot be presumed to exist in everyone.

A mixed society would be very poorly maintained on the basis of a moral world if one only flattered the senses with pleasant stimuli. For, even taking into account the vacuity of such provision, one could never be sure that the private taste of one individual member of society would not find repellent that which gave pleasure to another; and assuming that this would be resolved for everyone through sheer variety, it could not be said that the one *shared* the pleasure of the other, but that each would enjoy things for himself, and bury his feelings within.

But this society would not be much better satisfied if one supplied it with the profound truths of mathematics, physics or diplomacy, for interest in these matters rests upon a particular understanding that cannot be expected from every person. The merely sensuous man and the man of specialized learning are thus both unsuitable subjects for conversation, because both equally lack the ability of generalizing their private feelings, and making the general interest their own.

Notes

1. *If it is reason . . . Rousseau*: The motto quotes Jean-Jacques Rousseau's popular epistolary novel *Julie, ou La nouvelle Héloïse* (1761): 'Si c'est la raison, qui fait l'homme, c'est le sentiment, qui le conduit' (III 7).

FIRST LETTER

1. *the practical part of the Kantian system*: Immanuel Kant's *Groundwork of the Metaphysic of Morals* (*Grundlegung zur Metaphysik der Sitten*) of 1785 and his *Critique of Practical Reason* (*Kritik der praktischen Vernunft*) of 1788.

FOURTH LETTER

1. *Lectures on the Vocation of the Scholar*: Johann Gottlieb Fichte, *Einige Vorlesungen über die Bestimmung des Gelehrten* (Jena and Leipzig: Gabler, 1794).
2. *This pure man . . . unity*: This thought stands in rather sharp contrast to the just invoked *Lectures on the Vocation of the Scholar*. For Fichte argues in his second lecture that the state is a contingent means of human perfection, which in the end needs to become superfluous.

SIXTH LETTER

1. *contrast between . . . the Greeks*: This criticism of the negative effects of modern utilitarian culture and enlightenment

on individual greatness and virtue in sharp contrast to the Ancients invokes Jean-Jacques Rousseau. It is also the central theme of an article by Ludwig Ferdinand Huber (1764–1804), Schiller's friend from Leipzig, published in Schiller's journal *Thalia*. See L. F. Huber, 'Ueber moderne Größe', *Thalia*, 1 (1786), pp. 6–20, esp. pp. 10–14. For a similar argument see Georg Forster, 'Die Kunst und das Zeitalter', *Thalia*, 3 (1790), pp. 91–109.

2. *Greek . . . polyps*: German original: 'Polypennatur der griechischen Staaten'. The studies by Swiss naturalist Abraham Trembley (1710–84) on the freshwater polyp, nowadays called hydra, made a huge sensation in eighteenth-century science. Especially, Trembley's discovery of the polyp's ability to regenerate from cut-off pieces challenged the established clear-cut distinction between animals and plants.

3. *mechanically driven whole*: The state was frequently compared to a machine in eighteenth-century German thought.

4. *Eternally shackled . . . knowledge*: For this claim about the effects of functional differentiation on the individual in modern states compare Huber, 'Ueber moderne Größe', p. 13: 'Politics, the art of war, government – what have they become in a modern sense? Subtle, complex clockwork, where a thousand wheels mesh together. Fate and nature might have destined one among thousands to stand on top and to survey the whole from an eagle's perspective. Yet a thousand others, who through their powers could make the same claims as he does, are distributed among the thousand small wheels of the machine, and must spend their lives turning, each in his own, without ever gaining a perspective upon the whole.' (My translation – A.S.)

5. *passions of the flesh . . . those of the mind*: 'Venus Cytherea' and 'Venus Urania' in the German original. See Plato, *Symposium*, 180d.

6. *This antagonism of powers . . .*: Schiller employs Kant's idea of unsociable sociability as a driving force of human civilization. See Kant, 'Idea for a Universal History with a Cosmopolitan Aim' (1784), in *Kant's Idea for a Universal History with a Cosmopolitan Aim: A Critical Guide*, ed. Amélie Oksenberg Rorty and James Schmidt (Cambridge: Cambridge University Press, 2009), p. 13: 'The means nature employs in order to bring about the development of all their predispositions is their antagonism in society, insofar as the latter is in the end the cause of their lawful order. Here I understand by "antagonism" the unsociable sociability of human beings.' AA 8, p. 20.

SEVENTH LETTER

1. *humanity in the negro will be honoured*: Schiller refers probably to the abolition of slavery in the French Caribbean colonies on 4 February 1794.

EIGHTH LETTER

1. *the son of Saturn in the* Iliad: In contrast to other gods and goddesses, Zeus, the highest Greek deity and son of Kronos (Roman: Saturn), intervenes only indirectly in the Trojan War, observing from afar.
2. *his grandson with divine arms*: Achilles.
3. *A wise old man . . . sapere aude*: Immanuel Kant in his essay 'An Answer to the Question: What is Enlightenment?' ('Beantwortung der Frage: Was ist Aufklärung?') of 1784 quotes this famous phrase from Horace (*Epistles* 1, 2, 40). Schiller's idea of aesthetic education elaborates Kant's emphasis on the problem of the lack of moral resolve as a key obstacle to human progress: 'Enlightenment is man's emergence from his self-incurred immaturity. Immaturity is the inability to use one's own understanding without the guidance of another. This immaturity is self-incurred if its cause is not lack of understanding, but lack of resolution and courage to use it without the guidance of another. The motto of enlightenment is therefore: *Sapere aude!* Have courage to use your own understanding!' (Kant, *Political Writings*, ed. H. S. Reiss, trans. H. B. Nisbet (Cambridge: Cambridge University Press, 1991), p. 54). AA 8, p. 35.
4. *goddess of wisdom . . . Jupiter's head*: Minerva (Greek: Athena).
5. *philosophy its name*: Philosophy means literally 'love of wisdom' in ancient Greek.

NINTH LETTER

1. *Agamemnon's son*: Orestes avenges the death of his father, slaying his mother Clytemnestra and her lover Aegisthus.
2. *a Nero and a Commodus . . . building which lent them cover*: Nero Claudius Caesar Augustus Germanicus (37–68) and Marcus Aurelius Commodus Antoninus Augustus (161–92),

Roman emperors. The building Schiller refers to is the Colos-
seum, named after the nearby colossal statue of Nero and place
of bloody public spectacles.

TENTH LETTER

1. *They . . . praised*: The most prominent case of this line of thought
    in the eighteenth century was Jean-Jacques Rousseau. In the
    Discours sur les sciences et les arts of 1750 and other writings
    he attacked the fine arts in combination with luxury for spelling
    moral corruption and social inequality, and for destroying civil
    liberty.

2. *Even . . . republic*: Plato excluded the poets from his model of
    the best state (*Politeia/Republic*, 398a, b).

3. *And in fact . . . same*: Like Rousseau in the *Discours sur
    les sciences et les arts*, Schiller challenges the commonplace
    in republican and civic humanist thought that the arts and
    sciences flourish best under political liberty. Instead, Schiller
    argues, the decline of liberty coincides with the rise of the fine
    arts.

4. *Pericles and Alexander*: Pericles (*c*.495–429 BC), Athenian states-
    man; Alexander the Great (356–323 BC), King of Macedonia
    and conqueror of the Persian Empire.

5. *Phocion*: An Athenian statesman (*c*.402–*c*.318 BC), famous for
    his austere virtue, in the time of Athens's struggle to preserve
    its liberty against the kings of Macedonia. He was sentenced to
    death by drinking hemlock.

6. *oriental luxury . . . fortunate dynast*: The influx of wealth as
    a result of the Roman conquest of Syria and Asia Minor was
    repeatedly blamed for the corruption of republican liberty
    and Roman virtues. Schiller refers to the emperor Augustus
    (63 BC–AD 14), whose reign terminated the Roman republic.
    In his *Siècle de Louis XIV* of 1751 Voltaire praised the respec-
    tive (quasi-)monarchical reigns of Pericles, Augustus, Pope
    Leo X and Louis XIV of France as golden ages of the arts and
    sciences.

7. *the Abbasids*: Caliphs of Baghdad (750–1258); their name
    derives from Abbas ibn Abd al-Muttalib, uncle of the prophet
    Mohammed.

8. *the glorious Lombard League*: Alliance of north-Italian cities
    which existed from 1167 to the early thirteenth century.

TWELFTH LETTER

1. *material impulse*: *Sachtrieb* in the German original. Schiller replaced
    it with *Stofftrieb* in the second edition, of 1801. Schiller borrows the
    term *Trieb* in the sense of an independent and permanent striving of
    the 'I' from Fichte's *Science of Knowledge* of 1794. Fichte writes: 'We
    call impulse a self-generating striving that is fixed, determined, and
    something certain' (*Grundlage der gesammten Wissenschaftslehre,
    als Handschrift für seine Zuhörer* (Leipzig: Gabler, 1794), p. 282
    (§7)). According to Fichte, the *Trieb* produces feeling and thus makes
    the external world palpable to the self. Schiller, however, blends this
    transcendental meaning with the post-Cartesian psychological dual-
    ism of contemporary anthropology. Schiller's distinction between
    Sachtrieb and *Formtrieb* corresponds to the established distinction
    between man's sensuous and rational nature. His attempt to over-
    come this dualism in the notion of the playful impulse (*Spieltrieb*,
    see below) takes up an important anthropological debate of his
    time. The Leipzig philosopher-physician Ernst Platner (1744–1818)
    develops a similar triadic model of human impulses as Schiller in his
    influential *Neue Anthropologie für Aerzte und Weltweise. Mit beson-
    derer Rücksicht auf Physiologie, Pathologie, Moralphilosophie und
    Aesthetik* (Leipzig: Crusius, 1790). Platner distinguishes between an
    animal impulse (*thierische Trieb*), which is directed at our physi-
    cal well-being, a spiritual impulse (*geistiger Trieb*), and a genuinely
    human impulse (*menschlicher Trieb*), which is especially the sphere
    of aesthetics and moral feelings. Like Schiller's *Spieltrieb*, the human
    impulse is not really an independent impulse but rather a synthesis
    of the two others, in which spiritual impulse and animal impulse are
    mixed and balanced.
2. *formal impulse*: *Formtrieb* in the German original. See note 1.

FOURTEENTH LETTER

1. *playful impulse*: *Spieltrieb* in the German original. See Twelfth
    Letter, note 1.

FIFTEENTH LETTER

1. *Burke . . . Mengs*: Edmund Burke, *Philosophical Enquiry into the
    Origin of Our Ideas of the Sublime and Beautiful* (London, 1757);

German translation: 1773; Anton Raphael Mengs, *Gedanken über die Schönheit und den Geschmack in der Malerei* (Zurich, 1762).

2. *Juno Ludovisi*: A colossal marble head of the first century AD, which was part of the collection of Cardinal Ludovico Ludovisi (1595–1632). Johann Joachim Winckelmann praised the 'lordly beauty' of the head in his widely read *History of Ancient Art* of 1764. Many eighteenth-century writers and travellers to Rome shared this enthusiasm. Goethe possessed a copy of the *Juno Ludovisi* while staying in Rome in 1787 and 1788. Modern scholarship identifies the head as a presentation of Antonia Minor (36 BC–AD 37), the mother of Emperor Claudius, who had herself portrayed as Juno.

SIXTEENTH LETTER

1. *liquifying and energetic beauty*: *Schmelzende* and *energische Schönheit* in the German original. While preserving the transcendental unity of beauty as freedom in appearance, Schiller here reworks the established distinction between the beautiful and sublime in eighteenth-century aesthetics with respect to beauty's psychological effects in experience. The function of liquifying beauty is to relax the dominating impulse, while energetic beauty aims at strengthening the weaker impulse. The aim is a balance between the material and the formal impulse. Sociologically, this double function of beauty should, on the one hand, lead to a cultivation of raw passions among the less privileged classes. On the other hand, it should strengthen resolve to act according to the moral law among the refined elite. Schiller elaborates this idea first in the Letter to the Prince von Augustenburg of 11 November 1793 (Enclosure).

SEVENTEENTH LETTER

1. *excellent author of Principles of Aesthetics etc*: Schiller refers to *Grundsaetze der Aesthetik, deren Anwendung und künftige Entwickelung* (Erfurt: Keyser, 1791), written by his friend Karl Theodor von Dalberg (1744–1817), a member of the Illuminati order, administrator of Erfurt, designated successor of the archbishop of Mainz and as such future arch-chancellor of the Holy Roman Empire.

TWENTY-FIRST LETTER

1. *the beginning of the last letter*: Schiller actually means the beginning of the Nineteenth Letter.
2. See the Fourteenth and Fifteenth Letters in the second issue of *Die Horen*.

TWENTY-SECOND LETTER

1. *about the Messiah*: In the manner of the famous epic poem *Messiah* of 1748–73 by Friedrich Gottlieb Klopstock (1724–1803).
2. *in the manner of Anacreon or Catullus*: The Greek lyric poet Anacreon (*c.*582–485 BC) was known for his cheerful drinking songs, and the Latin poet Catullus (*c.*84–54 BC) was famous for his erotic poetry.

TWENTY-FOURTH LETTER

1. *Iphigenia in Tauris*: Freely quoted from Goethe's play *Iphigenie auf Tauris* of 1787 (lines 328–35).
2. *dogmatic eudaemonian systems*: In line with Kant's practical philosophy, Schiller rejects all systems of moral philosophy which centre on the idea of happiness as the highest good. This includes any theology which propagates happiness in the afterlife. Instead Schiller emphasizes the central value of moral freedom.

TWENTY-FIFTH LETTER

1. *Zeus . . . Saturn*: Zeus (Roman: Jupiter) overthrew the reign of his father Kronos (Roman: Saturn), a Titan and keeper of time, according to ancient Greek and Roman mythology. Kronos' reign is identified with the Golden Age of a carefree life for humankind.

TWENTY-SIXTH LETTER

1. *only the favour of chance . . . to beauty*: Schiller's sketch of a conjectural history of the human capacity to create works of

art, and thus to become a reflective and moral animal, emphasizes the contingency of human self-perfection. This ability, for Schiller, is the result of very specific geographical and historical circumstances, especially of the insular world of ancient Greece. He thus rejects the idea of divine providence or other teleological models of human history. Schiller's account of history here is very close to the philosophical narrative of history that Rousseau develops in the *Discours sur l'origine et les fondements de l'inégalité parmi les hommes* (or *Second Discourse*) of 1755. This narrative of human history, emphasizing contingency over providence, was usually associated with the notorious Epicurean philosophic poem, *De rerum natura* (*On the Nature of Things*) by Lucretius (*c.*99–*c.*55 BC).

2.   *Herder . . . History of Mankind*: Johann Gottfried Herder, *Ideen zur Philosophie der Geschichte der Menschheit*, vol. 3 (Riga and Leipzig, 1787), ch. 13. Schiller refers to Herder's claim that the maritime geography of Greece, featuring both openness and closure, favoured the development of a highly dynamic culture. For it allowed repose and activity, production and pleasure, as well as exchange and original development protected from foreign invasions.

3.   *olive wreath . . . purple cloak*: Schiller here contrasts the ancient symbol of virtuous merit with the symbol of inherited power.

4.   *aesthetic appearance*: The term denotes the man-created sphere of beauty and the fine arts, in which human freedom becomes palpable to us as sensuous creatures. It is sharply distinguished from moral or logical appearance as forms of deception. The concept is part of Schiller's attempt to counter Rousseau's critique of modern society as a canvas of mere moral appearances, which have caught the self in a net of dependencies on external recognition. Instead, aesthetic appearance becomes a liberating medium because it frees us from the pressure of material and psychic needs and generates reflection.

TWENTY-SEVENTH LETTER

1.   *Caledonian*: Member of a Celtic tribe in what became Scotland.
2.   *Trojan army . . . measured pace*: This description of the Greek and the Trojan armies is taken from Homer (*Iliad*, III, 1–9.) It was used as a standard example to illustrate the contrast between barbarians and civilized Greeks.

3. *dynamic state*: The *dynamische Staat* corresponds to the *Naturstaat* (natural state) in the Third and Fifth Letters. In this passage Schiller, however, emphasizes its character as a political institution, created to enforce rights claims.

4. *ethical state*: The *ethische Staat* corresponds to the moral state in the Third and Fourth Letters. Schiller here invokes and reworks a concept from Kant's *Die Religion innerhalb der Grenzen der bloßen Vernunft* of 1793–4, a work in which Kant refers very favourably to Schiller. The concept of an ethical state is essentially Kant's attempt to adopt the idea of the (invisible) Church for the purposes of his practical philosophy. The aim of this community is to mend and prevent the moral evil which arises from man's unsociable sociability. According to Kant, this community presupposes the existence of a political or lawful community: 'An association of human beings merely under the laws of virtue, ruled by this idea, can be called an ethical and, so far as these laws are public, an ethico-civil (in contrast to a juridico-civil) society, or an ethical community. It can exist in the midst of a political community and even be made up of all the members of the latter (indeed, without the foundation of a political community, it could never be brought into existence by human beings) . . . the ethical community can also be called an ethical state, i.e. a kingdom of virtue (of the good principle).' Immanuel Kant, *Religion Within the Boundaries of Mere Reason*, trans. and ed. Allen Wood and George di Giovanni, with an Introduction by Robert Merrihew Adams (Cambridge: Cambridge University Press, 1998), p. 106; AA 6, pp. 94–5. The comparison between the invisible Church of true believers and the aesthetic state is taken up in the final footnote.

5. *aesthetic state*: Schiller's hybrid triadic model of dynamic, ethical, and aesthetic state does not designate three independent or different forms of state. Instead, it can be understood best as three different functions or moments of the state in bringing about a fully human society.

6. *Taste . . . individual*: In the Letter to Augustenburg of 3 December 1793 Schiller had attributed the function of socialization to taste *and* religion, with the latter mainly aimed at the lower classes. Here, religion has been dropped from the argument, partly because taste is understood much less as a mere surrogate of virtue.

7. *Does . . . appreciation*: Schiller moved this footnote into the main body of the text in the second edition, of 1801, dropping the final two sentences, to give the essay a more rounded character.

In this version, it is standardly read as evidence of the elitist and eventually utopian character of Schiller's project – in social terms, a return to the Illuminati origins of the text. In light of the original version this interpretation is problematic. The footnote rather seems to indicate that these forms of aesthetic socialization do exist already, even if in small circles. Schiller planned to elaborate his concept of the aesthetic state in future writings but never succeeded. The term *pure Church* invokes the concept of the invisible Church from Augustine and the Protestant reformers of the sixteenth century. In contrast to the visible Church as a worldly institution, it denotes the community of the godly elect. The visible and the invisible Churches overlap but are not identical. Again, there are notable parallels to Kant's concept of the ethical community as a secular version of the invisible Church, which is in need of actualization through (imperfect) institutions, such as established religion. See note 4.

LETTERS TO PRINCE FREDERICK CHRISTIAN VON AUGUSTENBURG

1. *in his critique of aesthetic judgement*: Immanuel Kant, *Kritik der Urteilskraft* (*Critique of the Power of Judgement*) (first published 1790).
2. *A law . . . insurrection*: Schiller here refers to a law ascribed to the Athenian politician and legislator Solon (*c.*638–*c.*558 BC) forbidding neutrality in times of *stasis* (civil strife). See Plutarch, *Parallel Lives*, 'Solon', 20.1. The authenticity of this law is debated. Schiller had lectured on Solon's lawgiving as part of his lectures on universal history at Jena. The lecture was published in his journal *Thalia* in 1790 under the title 'The Legislation of Lycurgus and Solon' (Die Gesetzgebung des Lykurgus und Solon).
3. *If sense's . . . heaven*: These verses were presumably taken from earlier, now lost versions of Schiller's poem 'The Artists' of 1788–9.
4. *our Nordic age*: Schiller invokes the eighteenth-century notion of a Germanic age that begins with the destruction of ancient Greek and Roman civilization by Germanic tribes. This results in a rise of feudal monarchies and a shift of power and civilization from southern to northern and western Europe. A prominent formulation of this thesis can be found in Montesquieu's *Spirit of the Laws* of 1748. For Schiller, modern Germanic Europe has not fully overcome its barbaric roots, lacking the balanced serenity of Greek spirit.

5. *If art . . . barbarism*: This passage echoes a wider debate in Germany about the undesirability of having one dominating cultural centre but avoiding the danger of plunging into the anarchy of having no cultural models at all. See esp. Johann Wolfgang Goethe's 'Litterarischer Sansculottismus', *Die Horen* 2.5 (1795), pp. 50–56.

6. *including a printed article*: Schiller's 'On Grace and Dignity' ('Über Anmut und Würde'), printed in his *Neue Thalia*, 1793.

7. *Baggesen*: Jens Baggesen, a Danish poet (1764–1826); see Introduction, pp. xiv–xvi.

8. *my fatherland after many years of exile*: Schiller refers to his extended visit to his native Württemberg in late 1793 and early 1794. Schiller fled Württemberg in 1782 after Duke Carl Eugen (1728–93) had ordered his arrest.

9. *Graff in Dresden*: Anton Graff (1736–1813) was a famous portrait painter of his time. He painted both Frederick Christian von Augustenburg and Schiller.

10. *sapere aude*: See above, Eighth Letter, note 3.

11. *Scilicet . . . arte*: Ovid, *Ars Amatoria*, 3, 545 (*The Art of Love and Other Poems*, trans. J. H. Mozley, revised G. P. Goold (Cambridge, MA and London: Harvard University Press, 1979), pp. 156, 157).

12. *Didicisse . . . feros*: Ovid, *Ex Ponto* 2, 9, 47–8 (*Tristia. Ex Ponto*, trans. Arthur Leslie Wheeler, revised G. P. Goold (Cambridge, MA and London: Harvard University Press, 1988), pp. 362, 363).

13. *Fiat . . . mundus*: 'Let justice be done, though the world perish.'

14. *the pure daimonic flame*: Schiller uses 'daimonic' in the sense of spiritual or inspired by genius. Cf. his essay 'Ueber das Erhabene' ('On the Sublime'), NA 21, p. 46.

15. *Pelasgians*: Greek term to designate the inhabitants of the Aegean before the arrival of the Hellenic peoples.

16. *common sense*: German *Gemeinsinn*.

17. *Kant's Critique of Reason*: Immanuel Kant, *Kritik der reinen Vernunft* (*Critique of Pure Reason*) (first published 1781).

18. *Anna Komnene*: Anna Komnene, a Byzantine princess (1083–1153), reports this event in her *Alexiad*, book 1. She ascribes the prisoner's lack of resolve to divine intervention, appeasing his mind. Schiller had edited an excerpt from the *Alexiad* as part of his *Sammlung historischer Memoires* of 1790.

19. *Duke Leopold of Brunswick*: (1752–85), was a Prussian general and brother of Anna Amalia, the Duchess of Saxe-Weimar-Eisenach. His death in the floods of the Oder in April 1785 in an alleged attempt to save his fellow citizens was hailed by many contemporaries as a virtuous model of self-sacrifice.

Acknowledgements

Alexander Schmidt gratefully acknowledges the generous support of the Alexander-von-Humboldt Foundation, whose Feodor-Lynen-Fellowship allowed the completion of this edition in the congenial atmosphere of the University of Chicago's Committee on Social Thought. He is pleased to record his debt to Avi Lifschitz, Isaac Nakhimovsky, Eva Piirimäe, Andrei Pop, Sibylle Röth, Beate Agnes Schmidt, Anette Schmidt, David E. Wellbery and Joachim Whaley for their helpful comments, support and feedback. Simon Winder, as editor, and Keith Tribe, as translator, were true delights to cooperate with on this edition.

THE STORY OF PENGUIN CLASSICS

Before 1946 ... 'Classics' are mainly the domain of academics and students; readable editions for everyone else are almost unheard of. This all changes when a little-known classicist, E. V. Rieu, presents Penguin founder Allen Lane with the translation of Homer's *Odyssey* that he has been working on in his spare time.

1946 Penguin Classics debuts with *The Odyssey*, which promptly sells three million copies. Suddenly, classics are no longer for the privileged few.

1950s Rieu, now series editor, turns to professional writers for the best modern, readable translations, including Dorothy L. Sayers's *Inferno* and Robert Graves's unexpurgated *Twelve Caesars*.

1960s The Classics are given the distinctive black covers that have remained a constant throughout the life of the series. Rieu retires in 1964, hailing the Penguin Classics list as 'the greatest educative force of the twentieth century.'

1970s A new generation of translators swells the Penguin Classics ranks, introducing readers of English to classics of world literature from more than twenty languages. The list grows to encompass more history, philosophy, science, religion and politics.

1980s The Penguin American Library launches with titles such as *Uncle Tom's Cabin*, and joins forces with Penguin Classics to provide the most comprehensive library of world literature available from any paperback publisher.

1990s The launch of Penguin Audiobooks brings the classics to a listening audience for the first time, and in 1999 the worldwide launch of the Penguin Classics website extends their reach to the global online community.

The 21st Century Penguin Classics are completely redesigned for the first time in nearly twenty years. This world-famous series now consists of more than 1300 titles, making the widest range of the best books ever written available to millions – and constantly redefining what makes a 'classic'.

The Odyssey continues ...

The best books ever written

PENGUIN (🐧) CLASSICS

SINCE 1946